2.99

THE STORY
OF A PRISON

THE STORY
OF A PRISON

PETER SOUTHERTON

With a foreword by
Lord Wolfenden

OSPREY

First published in 1975 by
Osprey Publishing Ltd,
137 Southampton Street, Reading, Berkshire
Member company of the George Philip Group

Printed in Great Britain by Cox & Wyman Ltd,
London, Fakenham and Reading

FOREWORD

This book is an exemplary piece of local history. By patient and thorough research Mr Southerton has unearthed a great deal of evidence about the history of the various buildings which down the centuries have served as penal institutions for the population of Reading and its neighbourhood. And he has woven this material into an absorbing narrative, which in itself is a valuable contribution to the social history of this part of England.

But he has done more than that. The story of Reading's gaols is told in the perspective of national movements of thought in the treatment of offenders and national developments in the structure and administration of prisons. It is just as well that we should be reminded, by unvarnished local records, what our penal system did, a comparatively short time ago, to a fourteen-year-old who stole a pair of boots.

There will always be argument about the relative weight which correction, deterrence and reform should carry in any system which deals with law-breakers. What admits of no argument is the progress in conscience, understanding and humanity which the local and individual facts of Mr Southerton's book so vividly demonstrate.

WOLFENDEN

ACKNOWLEDGEMENTS

This book could not have been compiled without the kind co-operation of many people in whose care there are collections of manuscripts and other material relating to Reading's gaols. In particular I would express my gratitude to the following:

Mr R. A. Richards, Governor, H.M. Prison, Reading.

Miss A. Green, County Archivist for Berkshire for access to the records of the Berkshire Quarter Sessions and other valuable material.

Miss D. Phillips and the staff of the Reading Borough Reference Library for access to documents in the local history collection and for permission to reproduce many of the illustrations of the New County Gaol.

Mr D. T. O'Rourke, University of Reading Library.

Mr K. J. Major.

Mr F. C. Padley.

The Editor, *Evening Post.*'

Here, too, I would like to acknowledge the help and support afforded me by my friends and colleagues of the Berkshire Probation and After-Care Service and of H.M. Prison Service and to my wife for her patience in hearing all this read over many, many times.

PETER SOUTHERTON.

CONTENTS

ILLUSTRATIONS

*Illustrations marked * are reproduced by courtesy of the Editor,
the* Evening Post. *The old prints are reproduced by kind permission
of the Borough Librarian.*

1 A BRIEF HISTORY OF PRISONS

Prisons have existed from earliest times but it was not until comparatively recently that the penalty of imprisonment came to be accepted as a method of dealing with offenders and the gaol as a place of punishment and correction.

Until the end of the eighteenth century, the punishment for all serious crime was death whilst for lesser offences corporal punishment of varying severity, defamatory punishments such as exposure in the pillory or stocks and, in appropriate cases, the imposition of a fine were recognized as lawful. In such circumstances the function of the prison was to serve as a place in which the offender might be securely held until such time as he was required to stand trial.

In 1403 a Statute of Henry IV directed that Justices of the Peace should only commit to the Common Gaol, that in which the Sheriff of the County had authority. Until that time there were innumerable small gaols kept by municipal corporations, powerful landowners, noblemen or high dignitaries of the Church. There was no form of regulation or inspection and the patrons were free to lease the gaol to private individuals. It is recorded that in the early years of the reign of Richard II a prisoner who died in the private gaol of the Abbot of Reading had starved to death. The Coroner's jury, perhaps wisely, commented that it could not decide who ought to have fed him.

In course of time the authority for the upkeep and management of the prisons became vested in the Justices of the Peace. Major decisions relating to capital works, the appointment and payment of the Keeper and subordinate members of the staff and the like were taken by the Justices assembled at Quarter Sessions. General oversight of the gaol and matters relating to the day-to-day business of the establishment were left to a small committee of Visiting Justices.

The concept of the prison as a place of punishment can be said to originate from the Elizabethan Poor Law which permitted the setting up of Houses of Correction to provide work for the unemployed poor and in which able-bodied vagrants, idle apprentices, harlots and others felt to be on the fringe of crime might be corrected in their habits by laborious discipline. Whilst the Keeper of the Common Gaol sought to make life there as jolly as possible, especially for those who could pay, the House of Correction pursued a regime of reform and deterrence. It was not long before the Justices were to commit all kinds of petty offender to the House of Correction to undergo detention with hard labour, a practice which was legalized in 1720.

During the eighteenth century the Common Gaol and the House of Correction became almost completely assimilated although the law continued to provide that Debtors might only be detained in that part of the building designated the Gaol whilst vagrants were restricted to the House of Correction.

Throughout the eighteenth century, conditions in prisons throughout the land were very bad indeed. This was a time of callous and ineffective treatment not only for prisoners but also for those unsound in body or mind as well as those whose only crime was to be poor. Any secure building might be employed as a place of detention – the abbey Gateway at Abingdon, the monastery gateway at St Albans and the keep of the ruined Norman castle at Oxford are typical. There was no classification of inmates, tried and untried being herded together, neither was there segregation of the sexes. Food and drink was inadequate as was the supply of light and fresh air. Sanitation was in some instances non-existent with the result that gaol fever (typhus) and other contagious diseases were prevalent to the peril not only of the prisoners and of their keepers but to the public at large. The gaolers having paid their rent naturally required as large a return as possible on the outlay and to this end levied various fees and charges for such services as the provision of bedding, for accommodation in less crowded parts of the building and for the removal of shackles. In some instances prisoners were required to pay a fee to secure their release and there are instances on record of prisoners acquitted by the Court being taken back to prison until such time as the gaoler's account might be settled. A profitable source of income for the gaoler was from the sale of beer, wine and spirits often at exorbitant prices.

When John Howard became High Sheriff of Bedfordshire in 1773, he became so alarmed at what he saw in his own county gaol that he toured the country inspecting other prisons and, some four years later, published his findings under the title, *The state of the prisons in England and Wales*. He recommended the provision of secure, clean, cellular accommodation with the segregation of the men from the women, of debtors from the criminals. He advocated the classification of prisoners according to the nature of their criminality, the introduction of useful labour, the abolition of fees and charges and a prohibition of the sale of strong drink. He advised in the strongest of terms the appointment of honest, humane gaolers who were to be properly remunerated for their services. His views were politely received but speedy action was not forthcoming. Although an Act of Parliament of 1784 provided for the segregation of the sexes in prison and for the provision of separate cells this measure seems largely to have been ignored.

With the foundation of the colonies on the American continent it became common practice to reprieve prisoners under sentence of death if they agreed to be shipped to the New World, and in course of time Transportation became recognized as a legal sentence. Following the declaration in 1776 by the colonists of their independence, Transportation was no longer possible and other measures had to be devised. One solution to the problem was to house those prisoners who would formerly have been transported in prison ships known as hulks and to employ them on public works. These prison hulks became so notorious for their unhealthy conditions that in 1779 the Government authorized the building of a National Penitentiary for the accommodation of those prisoners who were the responsibility of the central Government. This institution was erected at Millbank on the site now occupied by the Tate Gallery. Its life was not however long as the opening up of Australia and Tasmania provided alternative overseas settlements for the disposal of convicts and the Millbank Penitentiary was abandoned. By the middle of the nineteenth century the citizens of Australia, like the Americans of earlier years, became increasingly reluctant to accept further convicts and in 1857 Transportation ceased for ever.

The final years of the system of transportation coincided with the abolition of the capital penalty for practically all offences other than murder and treason and it became apparent that convicted criminals had sooner or later to return to the community. The majority of the common gaols had little to commend them and there was much public discussion of the problem with considerable interest in fostering the reformative aspects of imprisonment. The prison administrators of the day, influenced in some measure by Quaker thought, felt that the most satisfactory way in which to induce a response to a measure of re-education, and to prevent contamination, was to keep the prisoners in solitary confinement thereby providing an opportunity for contemplation and repentance. The sincerity of their intentions is beyond dispute but the results were tragic and the effect is still to be felt.

To provide an environment superior to that which had hitherto existed in the local prisons, Parliament authorized the building of a prison designed especially to cater for the new regime and in April, 1840, the first stone of the 'New Model Prison' at Pentonville was laid. Pentonville and the prisons subsequently built to that plan offered strict cellular confinement. There was no need for workshops, classrooms or space for the prisoners to meet in association and, further, such an establishment could function with the minimum of staff. These buildings survive to house the majority of the prisoners of today.

Shortly before Pentonville opened, the Home Secretary, Sir Robert Peel, introduced his Gaol Act which obliged local authorities to adopt the Howard recommendations of some fifty years before and to submit quarterly reports to the Home Office concerning the administration of their prisons. This important piece of legislation also enforced the separation of debtors, untried prisoners and convicted prisoners from each other as well as setting standards for the size, ventilation and heating of the cells. A team of five Inspectors was appointed but such was the power of the Magistracy that no provision was made to enable the Government to enforce the recommendations of its own supervisory staff. The reports of the Inspectors were however laid before Parliament and defects in administration made public.

At this time two systems of discipline were in operation; the 'silent system' which permitted prisoners to work in association but in absolute silence and the 'separate system' under which prisoners were strictly segregated from each other. The former system was practised in the old Reading gaol, the latter in the new gaol which was constructed on the model of Pentonville. By 1863, the 'separate system' was adopted as the sole foundation of prison discipline in a deterrent regime affording 'hard labour, hard fare and hard bed'.

The Conservative Government returned in 1874 was committed to a reduction in the county rates and the centralization of prison administration was one means whereby this could be achieved. The Queen in her speech from the Throne in February 1876 refers to 'a measure for promoting economy and efficiency in the management of prisons and at the same time effecting a relief of local burthens'. The word became flesh in the Prisons Act of 1877 which effectively nationalized the prisons and transferred to the Home Secretary all responsibilities which had hitherto fallen to the Justices. A new body, the Prison Commission, was created to administer this very substantial undertaking.

Many of the Justices were reluctant to relinquish their powers and as a conciliatory gesture the Act provided that any Justice of the Peace who had jurisdiction in the area in which a prison was situated could visit the prison at any time, could inspect and could enter his observations in the Visitors' Book. There was also to be a Visiting Committee of Justices appointed by Quarter Sessions or by the Magistrates' Bench charged with the responsibility for the regular inspection of the prison, the responsibility to investigate and to report upon abuses and an obligation to listen to prisoners' applications and complaints, in private if necessary. The Visiting Committee was also vested with the power to hear disciplinary charges against prisoners and to award the appropriate punishment. These duties have remained substantially unchanged over the course of almost one hundred years.

For the convict prisons, Corrective Training and Preventive Detention establishments and for the modern central training prisons which have no close local connections a similar function is performed by the Board of Visitors which differs from the Visiting Committee only so far as the members are appointed by the Secretary of State and not by the Justices of the County; a proportion only are Magistrates, the remainder being selected from persons of good standing in the community.

The first Chairman of the Prison Commission was Sir Edmund Du Cane, a retired colonel of the Royal Engineers, the greater part of whose career had been spent in prison administration, albeit in the military setting. He undertook his duties with great competence. Under his control a uniform system of rules affecting both the prisoner and members of the prison staff was introduced. The number of prisons was reduced from 113 to 67. New and precise regulations concerning dietary were drawn up, sanitation was greatly improved and within a short time there was a noticeable reduction in the death rate among prisoners. The new regime was harsh, deterrence with economy being Du Cane's principal aim. He did, however, introduce an incentive to industry and good behaviour among prisoners

by initially placing the inmate in an unattractive environment and rewarding good response by the grant of additional
privileges.

The very rigidity of the system was to prove a handicap and
by 1894 the public had again become uneasy concerning the
state of the prisons, the incidence of tuberculosis among
prisoners, the repeated reconviction of men, and women too, who
had passed through the system and the alarming fact that altogether too many discharged prisoners were so broken in spirit
as to be incapable of earning an honest livelihood. A committee
under the chairmanship of Sir Herbert Gladstone, youngest son
of William Ewart Gladstone, was set up in 1895 to investigate
and to report upon the situation and its findings comprise one of
the most important and far-reaching documents in prison history. The final report condemned the approach to prisoners
which was at that time in vogue and laid down lines for prison
administration that have been followed to this day. Its essence
may be detected in the following extracts:

> The great and, as we consider, proved danger of this
> highly centralised system has been, and is one in which
> attention has been given to organisation, finance, order,
> health of the prisoners and prison statistics; the prisoners
> have been treated too much as a hopeless or unworthy
> element of the community, and the moral as well as the legal
> responsibility of the prison authorities has been held to
> cease when they pass outside the prison gates.

> We think the system should be made more elastic, more
> capable of being adapted to the special cases of the
> individual prisoners; that prison discipline should be more
> effectually designed to maintain, stimulate or awaken the
> higher susceptibilities of prisoners, to develop their moral
> instincts, to train them in orderly and industrious habits,
> and whenever possible turn them out of prison better men
> and women, both physically and morally, than when they
> came in.

The Gladstone Committee recommended the abolition of the treadwheel and other forms of unproductive labour, advocated the introduction of useful work and technical instruction in association, the reduction of time spent in cellular confinement and the segregation of habitual criminals from the less sophisticated.

Sir Edmund Du Cane retired about this time and was succeeded by Sir Evelyn Ruggles-Brise whose duty it became to put into effect the provisions of the Prison Act of 1898 which incorporated a great many of the Gladstone recommendations. One of the reforms introduced at this time was the grant of remission of sentence for good conduct for any prisoner serving one month or more.

The treatment of young offenders took a new direction over the course of the next few years. The year 1901, saw legislation whereby juveniles could be remanded to the care of some fit person instead of to prison. In 1908, an entirely new system of treatment for young offenders between the ages of 16 and 21, which had been pioneered at the former convict prison at Borstal, near Rochester, was sanctioned by Parliament. In the same year Preventive Detention, a form of custody for the criminal who is repeatedly guilty of offences and is neither deterred nor reformed by sentences of imprisonment, was also introduced.

The experience of the Suffragettes and of the Conscientious Objectors of the First World War forced an awareness of prison conditions upon a group of people who had a sense of public responsibility and who were both educated and vocal. Their criticism helped bring about further reform. In 1921, the traditional prison crop and the uniform bespattered with broad arrows, 'the dress of shame' were abolished, better arrangements were made for exercise, the restrictions upon visiting and correspondence were relaxed to some extent and a general, educational scheme for prisoners was introduced.

The outbreak of war in 1939 temporarily halted progress and brought stress the like of which had never previously been experienced even in the darkest days of the War of 1914–18. Not only was there a desperate shortage of staff to cope with an influx of new committals including enemy aliens and detainees under the Defence Regulations, there was also the very real danger from enemy action with which to contend. The Prison Service proved able to weather this severe storm, although traditions which had grown up over the course of the past century were swept away almost overnight.

The problems of overcrowding and understaffing persisted into the post-war years and continue to be felt to the present day. The process of reform was resumed and radical changes in the penal method have taken place over the course of the past twenty years. The concept of humane containment has given way to that of treatment, training and rehabilitation. Specialist staff in the field of medicine, psychiatry, education and social welfare have been brought into the prisons. Prison industry is now coordinated and developed under a Director with special responsibility in that field. The ultimate deterrent of corporal punishment for offences against prison discipline has been abandoned, the privilege of a short period of home leave to allow prisoners completing long sentences to renew family ties was introduced in 1951, whilst in 1953 selected prisoners were allowed the opportunity to work away from the prison in civilian employment as a step towards their rehabilitation and re-establishment in the community.

To accommodate a prison population which was at one time to exceed 42,000, a programme of new prison building and the conversion of former service camps for use as open and semi-open establishments has been embarked upon with a fervour rivalling that of the 1840s. Among the new prisons are the psychiatric establishment at Grendon Underwood near Aylesbury, the industrial complex at Coldingley near Bisley and purpose-built training prisons such as those at Blundeston and Gartree. A great deal of time and money has been spent modernizing and refurbishing a number of the older prisons, that at Reading being one.

The share of the national resources now afforded the Prison Service must reflect the degree of public knowledge, understanding and support of its work and also reflect something of the values of the nation, changed as they are from the days when Hawthorne could write of 'the black flower of civilized society – a prison'.

WANTED at the County Gaol and Bridewell at
Reading immediately, a steady honest and sober
middle aged MAN, who can bear confinement, as
an ASSISTANT TURNKEY, at the said Gaol: if he
is a married man he cannot be accommodated
with apartments for his family; he will
himself be expected to sleep at the Gaol,
and never to absent himself therefrom without
leave. A single, middle aged man, without
incumbrances would be preferred: he must
give a reference for character; if by letter,
the postage to be paid, to the Keeper of the
said Gaol. The wages will be 18s. per week.

– Advertisement for assistant turnkey, *Reading
Mercury,* 28 January 1822.

The original County Gaol stood in Castle Street on the site now
occupied by St Mary's Church. The year in which this prison
was established is uncertain but the registers of the Parish
Church of St Mary the Virgin provide evidence of its existence
during the latter quarter of the sixteenth century. The Register
of Burials records the interment on 10 January 1571 of 'Newman,
a felon hanged'. Subsequent entries record the burial on 11 June
1579, of 'William Mortine, a prisoner' and on 7 July 1585, of
'John Greenwoode, pressed to death'. The latter had suffered the
hideous penalty imposed upon prisoners who, when brought
before the Assizes on a charge of felony, refused to enter a plea
as in the event of a conviction their lands and property would
be forfeit to the Crown leaving their dependants destitute. In

order to extract a plea, the unfortunate prisoner would be taken to the gaol where he would be stretched upon the floor and weights 'as heavy as he can bear and more' piled upon his body until he submitted or expired. To add to his torment, the law provided that the prisoner whilst subject to this torture which was referred to in the Court rolls as *'peine fort et dure'* should be allowed 'but three morsels of coarse barley bread' and to drink, 'water from the gutter nearest the gaol' and these on alternate days. The Baptismal Register records the Christening on 16 January 1574 of 'John Nabb borne in prisone', whilst in April, 1602, we read of 'Christian, a base child borne at the gayle'. An early entry in the Register of Marriages records the wedding on 22 April, 1683, of 'Richard Marshall and Mary Elton from ye Goale'.

The building which was very small – the site measuring only 100 ft by 90 ft after the premises had been enlarged in the eighteenth century – served chiefly as a place of remand for persons awaiting trial who, unable to find sureties, were obliged to remain in custody and for those already sentenced and awaiting their fate. Debtors, too, were imprisoned here.

Although the doors were strong and the windows barred, the principal means of security was the use of fetters, iron collars and chains. The facilities afforded the inmates were minimal, prisoners prior to the nineteenth century being obliged to fend for themselves. Those without private means or sympathetic friends had to rely upon such assistance as the Poor Law might provide. The Keeper of the gaol was not salaried and relied for his living upon monies received from the prisoners committed to his safe-keeping and from his trading activities. One such official, when asked why the prisoners did not even have straw upon which to sleep, replied to the effect that any such luxuries would have to come from his own pocket.

In 1720, the prisoners in the County Gaol complained bitterly that the Keeper not only treated them cruelly but added insult to injury by charging exorbitant prices for their lodgings and provisions. Although exonerated of the charges of ill-usage it was found that the prices asked by the Keeper were excessive but it was not until 1731 that a table of rules and fees was drawn up and openly displayed:

1. Prisoners are to send for beer, ale and victuals from what place they may please.

2. They are free to use bedding, linen and other necessaries as they think fit without having them purloined.

3. Two prisoners in one bed pay 1s. 6d. a week; for a single bed 2s. 6d. a week chamber rent.

4. Those who provide their own bedding to pay 1s.

5. The Keeper to sell beer in sealed pots.

6. No felon to share a bed with a debtor without the consent of the latter.

7. Prisoners for debt only to use the Mumping Room. Charity there collected to be distributed amongst those actually begging there.

8. No dogs nor pigeons to be kept in the gaol.

9. One shilling to be paid to the Gaoler on delivery of declaration against any prisoner.

10. Every debtor and felon to pay on his discharge 13s. 4d. to the Keeper and 2s. 6d. to the Turnkey.

About this time the gaol was enlarged to accommodate some 20 prisoners in comparative comfort but this number was often exceeded. John Howard records that on the occasion of his visit in April, 1779, there were detained in addition to 9 felons and

9 debtors no less than 19 men impressed for service in the Royal Navy and awaiting escort to Spithead.

Of the Gaol, Howard writes:

> Debtors and felons have their courts separated by iron rails. The former have a kitchen; and for the Master's side, many rooms but no free yard. Felons have a day room for men and women. The night room for men is a large dungeon down four steps; the prisoners broke out lately. A separate night room for women. The Turnkey now has a lodging room over the felons' dungeon with an alarm bell so that an escape will be more difficult. There is lately a small room fitted up as an infirmary. There is a room used for the Gaoler's poultry. No straw. The common side debtors pay 1s. 6d. a week, the Master's side 2s. 6d. for lodging. Outside the gaol were verses appealing to the charity of passers by.

By the turn of the century the Gaoler was allowed the sum of 3d. per head per day from County funds to feed and to maintain the convicted felons. There was no such provision for the debtors who were required not only to cater for themselves but had still to pay for their accommodation according to a scale of charges laid down by Quarter Sessions. During the latter years of the eighteenth century these were as follows:

In the Sheriff's or Master's Ward (finding his own bedding)	1s. per week
With bedding provided by the County	2s. 6d. per week
For a room in the Keeper's house	2s. 6d. per week

A debtor could arrange to have his own food, clothing and bedding sent in if he so required and was also permitted to purchase a daily allowance of a pint of wine or a quart of beer, the latter not to exceed 1d. per quart in price. To support himself and his family and presumably to assist towards discharging his debt, he might follow his normal employment in prison provided the materials and tools were acceptable to the Gaoler. Of the proceeds of this labour, one third was appropriated by the Gaoler.

If a debtor was completely without means and had no friend or relative willing or able to help him out, life in prison must have been pretty bleak. Accommodated in the Common Ward, the less fortunate were obliged to beg assistance of passers by. Those obliged to seek a living in this way were permitted the use of the Mumping Room, a small chamber with a grating opening on to Castle Street. Above was a board bearing the verse to which Howard refers:

> Oh ye whose hours exempt from sorrow flow
>> Behold the seat of pain, and want, and woe;
> Think while your hands th'entreated alms extend
>> That what to us ye give, to God ye lend.

It would however seem that the debtors were not always tactful in their approach to the public and in 1791, following repeated complaints concerning their demeanour and language, the Quarter Sessions upon the recommendation of the Visiting Justices ordered that they should no longer solicit public charity. It was accordingly arranged that any donations should be received by the Gaoler who would henceforth keep proper books of account and that monies collected in this way should be disbursed at the discretion of the Chaplain.

By the middle of the eighteenth century it was apparent that the gaol was not only inadequate for its purpose on account of overcrowding but that it was rapidly falling into a state of disrepair. In 1783, we find the High Sheriff and Grand Jury of the County of Berkshire petitioning Parliament to the effect that they 'in common with the rest of the Kingdom have suffered during the late war by the difficulties which have arisen in inflicting the due and accustomed punishment on offenders not sentenced to die . . . their gaol is inconveniently full of convicts, from whence much danger arises of escapes and of infectious distempers that may spread'.

At the Michaelmas Sessions of 1791 after much careful discussion it was resolved unanimously that 'the present County Gaol on account of its bad state of repair and the communication existing between the debtors and the felons which cannot be remedied, is improper and unfit for further repair and addition'. The Castle Street site did not permit of expansion and an alternative site had to be found. It was ultimately agreed that the existing House of Correction which had been erected as recently as 1785 at the eastern end of the Forbury should be enlarged and adapted.

The architect commissioned to undertake the building of the new establishment, which was to incorporate the improvements advocated by John Howard, was Robert Furze Brettingham of Princes Street, Hanover Square, London. Aged 41 years and born plain Robert Furze, this gentleman had some years previously become related by marriage to the Brettinghams, a family boasting among its members several architects of distinction and 'supposing professionally that it might be of advantage to him' adopted their surname. A year previously, upon the death of Thomas Blackburn, a noted prison architect, he had succeeded to most of that colleague's practice. He was already known locally, having built the handsome High Bridge across the Kennet, a structure which survives to the present day.

Tenders were invited for the contract to build a two-storey block with accommodation for 30 felons and a similar number of debtors together with a chapel, Keeper's house and usual offices. Of the three applicants, William Collier, builder of Reading, offered to undertake the task for £3,020 whilst Messrs Storer and Fisher of Grosvenor Square asked £2,806. The lowest, and most acceptable tender was that of William Wingate, carpenter of Lower Street, Islington, who indicated that he could carry out the work for only £2,480. Unfortunately, before the necessary documents could be signed, Wingate discovered that he had miscalculated and asked leave to raise his tender. To this suggestion the County would not agree. Storer and Fisher having withdrawn, the contract was finally awarded to Collier who agreed to carry out the work for £3,000.

Collier was offered the services of the prisoners in a labouring capacity but elected to employ local workmen selected by himself. Convict labour was, however, utilized for heavy and uncongenial tasks such as site clearance, road making and the digging of foundation trenches and sawpits.

The work went ahead smoothly, Mr Brettingham from time to time authorizing payment to the builder in respect of work completed. The site being situated on gravel, the groundwork presented few problems. The feature which presented the greatest difficulty was the solid and enduring nature of the foundations of the former Reading Abbey which the builders all too frequently encountered. So solid were these flint walls that the traces once more uncovered during the rebuilding operations of 1971 resisted the assault of modern power tools and had to be cut away by hand, one stone at a time. Part of the site, it was discovered, had served as the burial ground of the Abbey and human remains were found in such abundance that the trenches for the footings had to be taken to a considerably greater depth than had originally been anticipated.

The Justices kept a close watch over the progress of the work and permitted little deviation from the approved plan. They rejected the builder's suggestion that toilet facilities should be omitted from the cells on account of the insufficiency of the water supply and that 'tubs or pans be used instead'. They ordered that the interior of the cells should be painted with 'lacquer in a light colour'. The Keeper was consulted as to the site of the place of execution and the drop was accordingly installed on the roof at the west end of the gaol, beneath which was a small paddock from which the public might obtain a good view of the proceedings.

The building was ready for occupation by September, 1793, and the felons transferred from the old gaol. The debtors were to remain at Castle Street until 1796 when the site was advertised for sale by auction. Regardless of their views publicly expressed

as to the decaying state of the buildings, the Justices nevertheless advertised the premises as 'the greater part new within
these past 27 years . . . very substantial and may easily be converted into Dwelling-houses, Store-houses or a Manufactory'.

Mr Brettingham authorized the payment to William Collier of
the final instalment of his account. All that now remained was
for him to collect the balance of his fees.

The Justices were unfortunately not altogether pleased by the
workmanship of their new gaol. A committee appointed to
examine the building reported that the roof admitted rain in
such quantities that not only were the upper cells wet and un-
inhabitable but that the water ran down the stairs into the lower
rooms. The privies in the cells – which were indeed incorporated
against all advice – were found to be unusable and very offensive. The archway of the southern gateway was said to be in
such a shaky state that its collapse was imminent whilst the gate
itself was but lightly panelled and quite insecure. Within the
building the iron plating that should have been firmly affixed
to floors, doors and other parts vulnerable to attack, had not been
properly mounted. Adding that the screws could be withdrawn
as easily as nails due to the softness of the boards beneath, it was
their view that inferior materials had been employed. We shall
see in a later chapter how a defective lintel contributed to an
escape from the condemned cell.

The Court recorded its displeasure of Mr Brettingham's
carelessness in supervising the building work by ordering the
withholding of a sum of £138. 12s. due to him by way of out-
standing fees. It was further resolved 'that Mr Brettingham be
never employed again by the County'. Despite this professional
setback the architect was called upon to design and build gaols
at Northampton, Poole and Downpatrick and from 1794 until
1805 held the office of Resident Clerk to the Board of Works.
The builder had by this time been paid in full but was penalized
by the refusal of the County to meet an additional account for
£216 5s.

It was left to the Keeper to arrange for the premises to be

made weatherproof by the re-pitching of the roof. He was also required to have the walls and floors strengthened. A local plumber by the name of Moore was called upon to 'place stink traps under the pipes of the necessaries'.

These privies were a source of trouble from the outset and the Surgeon in his reports repeatedly warned against the risk of disease from them but it was not until 1828, some 35 years after their installation, that they were removed and the nuisance eliminated. It was not the unhealthy atmosphere, however that caused the authorities to seal up the drains and to supply close stools in their place but a discovery on the part of the Visiting Justices that the outlet pipes offered a direct communication with the *'Cloaca maxima'* of the gaol affording an easy though far from agreeable channel of escape to the Kennet. There is, however, no record of any prisoner having made his escape by that route.

It has not proved possible so far to trace any illustration of the old gaol and no vestige of that building now remains, all having been swept away when the Victorian Prison was erected. The written descriptions that have come down to us show the old gaol to have been a low, solid structure of red local brick. The building in its original form was symmetrical and not un-attractive, its austere façade relieved by a turret clock above the Keeper's house which guarded the main entrance.

The local historian, John Man, in his guide to the Reading of 1810 entitled *The stranger in Reading* says of the gaol:

At the eastern end of the Forbury is the County Gaol and Bridewell, a modern brick building on Mr Howard's plan. In the front is the Keeper's house and at a small distance behind is a very neat chapel. The rest of the building in the form of a square contains the different wards and cells which are furnished with every necessary convenience that can be expected in such places.

Behind the wards is a large courtyard surrounded by a high wall but open to the sun; here the prisoners occasionally

walk. . . . Round the outer wall of the prison is a garden
enclosed by another wall but lower where some of the
convicts are occasionally employed.

The prisoners are dressed in party coloured clothes half
blue, half yellow from head to foot except the shoes.

Subsequent development destroyed the clean lines of the
original building. Intended to accommodate some 60 prisoners,
the number of committals during the early years of the nineteenth century outstripped the estimate of the County Justices
and the premises were soon seriously overcrowded. In 1824, the
building was extended along the western side to provide accommodation for a growing number of female prisoners. A new
bakehouse was erected in 1826. The following year it became
necessary to provide a new Debtors' Ward. The siting of the
latter building was unfortunate from the point of view of the
prison authorities as the windows of the upper storey overlooked
the garden of the Matron's house which was used by the female
debtors as an airing yard and by other women prisoners to hang
out their washing. Such is the frailty of human nature that there
were frequent complaints of breaches of the rule of silence and
of undue familiarity between the men and the women.

By January, 1830, the Visiting Justices were complaining to
Quarter Sessions that there were now 142 prisoners accommodated in a gaol intended for no more than 100 inmates. The
following year, a period of considerable disturbance in the rural
areas, saw up to 250 prisoners in custody. It being impossible to
cope with such a population, arrangements were made with the
Reading Corporation for all the women prisoners to be transferred temporarily to the Borough Bridewell in Friar Street.
Later it became necessary also to transfer a party of male
prisoners to ease the still intolerable overcrowding.

In 1830, Augustus Schuts, a former Magistrate and Visiting
Justice, bequeathed in trust to the County the not inconsiderable
sum of £1,000 for the erection within the gaol of separate
buildings 'for the confinement of persons committed there for

idleness or slight offences'. After careful deliberation it was decided to employ the legacy towards the cost of providing an infirmary and separate accommodation for young male offenders. No action was taken towards the provision of quarters for female juvenile offenders as it was felt that so few girls were sent to prison that those received could easily receive proper care and supervision in the existing women's wards.

Sir William Cubitt, whose services as architect had earlier been sought, was consulted and an acceptable plan prepared for a project which it was estimated would cost about £2,000. The preparation of the necessary designs and specifications proved slow and tedious as the architect whose home was in Lowestoft found it inconvenient to travel too frequently to Reading. His plans having been approved, the Justices dispensed with his services and appointed in his place Richard Billinge of Reading. Tenders were invited and the contract awarded to George Ball who commenced work in June, 1832. The same contractor also extended the boundary wall of the prison to enclose an area of land between the existing south wall and the Kennet which had been acquired for further expansion of the gaol.

A treadmill was introduced in 1822. Invented by Sir William Cubitt some four years previously, Reading was one of the first prisons to employ this device for the harnessing of the energies of prisoners sentenced to undergo hard labour. Unlike the tread-wheel which was later to be installed in the majority of the prisons throughout the country, the Reading treadmill was a fully productive flour mill operated by prisoner power.

Erected by Messrs Penn, millwrights of Greenwich, at a cost of £1,700, the motive power for the millstones and other machinery was provided by the efforts of a team of 32 prisoners 'climbing' a wooden barrel upon which were steps spaced about 7 in. apart. It was estimated by the authorities that during the course of a working day of ten hours, each man would climb this endless staircase to the equivalent of 13,300 feet.

The wheels were housed in a two-storey building some 33 ft

in length divided into four compartments for ease of control of the prisoners. Above the wheel compartments were four rooms, one fitted for the storage of inmates' clothing and personal property, the remainder for general storage purposes. An inventory compiled in 1836 shows these to have contained a varied assortment of old junk including articles of disused furniture, old firegrates, tools, scrap iron, a bundle of javelin staves and a quantity of old fetters. The mill proper was of three storeys. At ground level was the Miller's office, above was the machinery and the dressing floor whilst the upper storey provided storage for grain and meal.

The mill was brought into use on Friday, 15 November, 1822. This novel form of employment was by no means welcomed by the prisoners who by midday on the following Monday were in a state of mutiny demanding better provisions and the issue of leather shoes in place of their usual wooden-soled footwear, failing which they would refuse to perform. It is reported in the *Reading Mercury* of that week that the Keeper and his assistants were hard put to it to restore order but that after some hesitation the prisoners returned reluctantly to work. As a result of this incident, the Gaoler was obliged to relay his concern to Quarter Sessions with a request for additional assistance 'for a better mode of security against general revolt'. His representations were met by the appointment of an additional Turnkey. It was further ordered that the windows of the wheel compartments be fitted with iron bars and that the doors should henceforth be locked whilst the prisoners were at work. To make conditions a little easier for the Turnkeys detailed to supervise the mill, sentry boxes were provided on either side of the building. Work at the treadmill was carried out in strict silence, the usual penalty for talking or other misbehaviour being three days' cellular confinement on a diet of bread and water.

The treadmill was highly unpopular and prisoners would go to almost any length to avoid this form of labour. So often did they complain that they were too unwell or too infirm to work that the Surgeon understandably became very cynical when his prisoner patients reported sick. Not only did they go out of their way to bring about symptoms of apparent illness by such means as swallowing soap which would produce an upset stomach and mild fever or by whitening the tongue with chalk. They would also aggravate old sores and wounds. Anyone even suspected of malingering would be referred to the Keeper and severely punished. It was not until 1828 however that there was another general refusal to work. On that occasion the Visiting Justices were called upon to reinforce the Keeper's authority by inflicting collective and individual punishments.

The management of the mill was the responsibility of the Miller, a Mr Cordery, who was employed at a weekly wage of £1 1s. He was also a baker with the responsibility of keeping the prison supplied with bread, an arrangement which lasted until the Summer of 1829 when it was found that the price of bread had fallen to such an extent that the saving originally made by baking on the premises could no longer be maintained. It was estimated at this time that the money saved amounted to a mere 7d. on 140 loaves.

The Miller was assisted in his task by one of the more trustworthy prisoners. In their report to the Midsummer Sessions of 1824, the Visiting Justices speak highly of one of these:

We report that Benjamin Bullock convicted at the Epiphany Sessions of 1823 of Poaching in the Night and sentenced to two years' hard labour has distinguished himself by his general good conduct and in particular has been employed from the 13th April 1823 up to the present time as an Assistant to the Miller and has uniformly conducted himself with diligence, civility and fidelity and has in all respects set a good example to the other prisoners.

For many years it fell to the Keeper to ensure that the mill remained in full production. In this matter he was faced with two problems, the occasional shortage of manpower to operate the machinery and, from time to time, a shortage of corn to be ground. On several occasions the Visiting Justices were moved to complain that the mill was standing idle for want of able-bodied men and on one occasion at least it was necessary to send to Abingdon Gaol for suitable labour. There were frequent demands that local poachers and vagabonds should be sent to the mill but this could not be legally enforced.

To keep the mill fully occupied and to relieve the Keeper of the time-consuming and inappropriate task of visiting Reading Market to tout for custom, the County Justices in 1828 entered into a contract with Samuel Slaughter, a local baker and corn merchant. It was agreed that upon Slaughter making available sufficient grain to keep the mill in constant use it would be ground and dressed for him at the favourable rate of 11s. per load for wheat, 10s. for barley, peas and beans. It was further agreed that all flour for use in the Gaol would be purchased from him.

About this time arrangements were made to improve the water supply to the various parts of the Gaol. Under Cubitt's supervision a set of three-throw lift pumps were installed in a small building adjoining the mill. These were so devised that they could be operated by a party of from four to ten men operating a crank or, alternatively, by coupling to the machinery of the treadmill. Whilst the apparatus operated very efficiently when powered by the crank, difficulties were experienced when it was linked to the treadmill. Such was the vibration that it was feared the wheel would be damaged. This problem was eventually resolved by fitting a set of balance weights to the pump mechanism.

It was discovered in 1834, that the mill was operating at a loss. Whilst this was due in the main to defective if not fraudulent accounting on the part of the Governor, Thomas Eastaff, it was also felt that the terms of Mr Slaughter's contract were weighted a little too heavily in his favour. It was accordingly resolved that the existing contract should be determined and tenders sought from persons prepared to offer more advantageous terms but few tradesmen expressed any interest and Samuel Slaughter's contract was renewed for a term of three years. The mill contract was again put to tender in 1837. On this occasion Slaughter was no longer interested and withdrew. Of those who tendered, none would accept the contract without the concessionary right to supply the gaol with bread, a condition to which the County would not agree. The mill, it seemed, was doomed to stand idle.

Governor Eastaff having resigned, it was suggested by his successor, Lieut Edward Hackett, R.N. that the treadwheel should be modified by disconnecting the mill machinery and the substitution of a friction brake thereby converting it to the orthodox punitive apparatus. The cost of the conversion he ascertained would be a mere £27 17s. and he went on to argue that not only would this modification obviate the cost of repairs to the mill machinery which had of recent years exceeded the total income from the rent and profits but, further, the knowledge that the effort involved was non-productive would render it all the more irksome to the prisoners. The apparatus did not however function at all smoothly in this form. Only when it was reconnected to the machinery of the mill, which acted as a form of flywheel, was the barrel able to rotate smoothly. In this form the treadwheel continued to operate until 1841 when the site was cleared to make way for the new county gaol. Offered for sale by public auction the treadwheel and the remaining fittings were sold for the modest sum of £61, the value of its scrap iron content.

To the right of the Forbury Road entrance and extending along the eastern side of the gaol was a range of small buildings, some of brick construction, some of wood. Among the principal of these were the bakehouse of 1826, with a bread store adjoining. Near by was the van house in which was kept the caravan employed for the conveyance of prisoners between the gaol and the Courts; alongside were a small but well-equipped forge and workshop, and stabling for three horses. A row of small sheds built against the outer wall were used for the storage of firewood and bulky materials.

Embodied in the premises but independent of the prison was

the guard room and armoury of the Berkshire Militia; as secure a place as any for the storage of firearms and ammunition, particularly in times of trouble. It is recorded that in March, 1816, a time of general unrest and depression following the Napoleonic War, when Basingstoke had been half destroyed by the mob rioting in protest against the Corn Laws, and when even the loyalty of the local militia was suspect, the Home Secretary ordered that their bayonets and the locks of their muskets should be lodged in the County Gaol.

Despite the lack of room within the gaol, there was an abundance of space outside the wall. Originally cultivated to provide vegetables for the consumption of the prisoners, the gardens were developed by Thomas Eastaff. His pride and joy was an ornamental garden fronting Forbury Road. So elaborate was this area with its brick paths, herbaceous borders and flowering trees and shrubs that the less charitable of his critics asserted that he spent more time there than in the prison. There was also a well-stocked orchard which in 1834, was reported to contain no less than 69 apple trees, 10 pear trees, 7 peach trees, 5 grape vines, 200 red and white currant bushes and 3 asparagus beds. From the reports of the prison dietary of the time it is clear that none of the produce found its way to the prisoners' table. Upon Mr Eastaff's resignation in October of that year, the value of the stock was agreed at £34 19s.

3 THE BRIDEWELL, THE COMPTER AND 'THE HOLE'

By virtue of its Borough status, the town of Reading had until the local government and county Boundary reforms which came into effect in April, 1974, independence of government from the County of Berkshire, the conduct of civic affairs being the responsibility of the Mayor and Corporation while the maintenance of law and good order was the province of Justices of the Peace selected from the more substantial and respectable of its citizens.

Prior to the nineteenth century, offenders ordered by the local Magistrates to be held in custody were rarely sent to the County Gaol but were committed to one or other of the prisons maintained at the expense of the ratepayers of the Borough. Of these the most ancient was the Compter Gateway of the Abbey. The western entrance to the Abbey precincts, this gateway until its demolition in the early years of the nineteenth century spanned the roadway to the south of St Laurence's church and was originally the Abbot's prison in which monks guilty of serious misconduct or insubordination were confined, as well as malefactors from the town. Today nothing remains although the site is marked by a small plaque on the wall of the church. The prisoners, well fettered for security, were lodged in three small rooms above the archway under the supervision of a single gaoler who lived in the Compter House adjoining.

From the early years of the seventeenth century this building appears to have been used principally for the accommodation of debtors and civil prisoners. The records of the Corporation show numerous committals to the Compter (or Counter as it was originally known) of persons failing to afford the Mayor and

Corporation the respect that those worthies considered their due:

17th June, 1646. Richard Hine sent to the Counter for treating the Mair and Company with contempt.

5th August, 1646. Edward London for using reproachful words of the Company and refusing to put in suertye for his good behaviour committed to the Counter.

There was room, too, in the Compter for members of the fair sex as the following entry, also for 1646, indicates:

This Day Mr Maior committed Goodwife Lovejoy's daughter to counter for jearing and scoffing Mr George Woldridge, Alderman.

Upon the Corporation being deprived in the eighteenth century of the power granted by Charter to enforce the payment of small debts, this prison fell into disuse. It would seem also that critics of the town council were by that time less likely to be thrown into prison.

Convicted felons and persons held in custody on suspicion or to await trial for criminal offences were detained in a more conventional prison situated in the nave of Greyfriars Church, Friar Street. This building was originally the conventual church of the Brethren of St Francis, the Grey Friars, who arrived in Reading in the year 1233 and who, in 1285, were granted an area of land at what was then the extremity of the town upon which to build their settlement. Following the dissolution in 1539 of the religious establishments of the country, the Friary was divided up and the church given to the Corporation for use as a town hall. In the early years of the seventeenth century it was used as a hospital and in 1631 became the local House of Correction wherein were housed the poor and the profligate.

Writing in 1810, John Man, a local historian, describes the prison as 80 ft by 54 ft in dimension comprising the original nave and side aisles of the church. The chancel had been taken down some years previously. The nave was open to the sky having

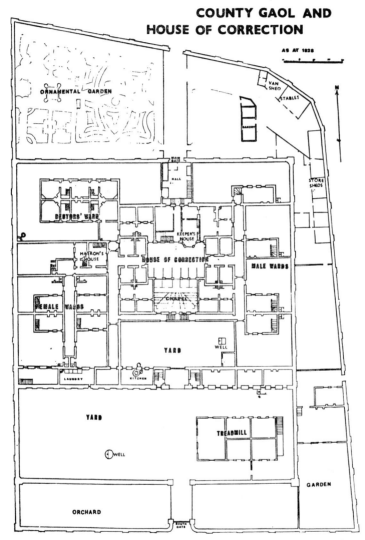

(From a plan of 1828)

in that year been dismantled as it had fallen into decay and was in danger of collapse. The area was divided by a transverse wall into two wards, one for male inmates, the other for females. The prisoners were accommodated in four cells in the north aisle where wooden partitions had been constructed between the pillars. Projecting from the north wall of the building was a block comprising three solitary cells each measuring 14 ft by 6 ft opening from a yard no more than 7 ft square. The only source of light and air was a small grille in the cell door, the only furniture a bed of straw. Here, as in the body of the prison, there was no provision for heating, neither was there any source of clean water.

There was no infirmary or sick room, neither is there any record of there being a kitchen or facilities for the preparation of hot meals. It is, of course, possible that gruel or soup for the prisoners may have been prepared in the Keeper's own kitchen.

The Keeper occupied a four-roomed cottage on the south side of the prison opening on to the street. There was no ready means of communication between the cottage and the prison and to attract attention the prisoners were obliged to kick upon the door between the prison and the Keeper's back yard. Adjacent to the Keeper's quarters, on the site of the present south transept, was a public-house, 'The Pigeons'.

The entire gaol is said to have been dark, damp and insanitary with the brick floor of the central courtyard green and slippery with slime. Conditions here must have defied description when in 1831 the Borough Justices agreed to accommodate the overflow of prisoners from the County Gaol which had become grossly overcrowded due to the sudden influx of prisoners committed for their part in the agricultural riots which had swept the county during the winter months of the previous year.

In a scathing report laid before Parliament in 1837, the Inspector of Prisons said of the Reading Bridewell that the only habitable accommodation there amounted to three cells. Whilst the majority of prisoners sent there were offenders sentenced by the local Justices to short terms of imprisonment without hard labour, debtors and persons held in custody pending committal, few of whom were held for more than a few days, conditions were nevertheless unsatisfactory in the extreme. He found that on one occasion as many as 6 persons were confined in a single cell.

The rebuilt County Gaol offering accommodation for as many prisoners as the Justices of the Borough cared to commit, the Mayor and Corporation in 1850 entered into a contract with the County to receive these at a charge of £6 per cell per annum plus a proportion of the cost of staffing and maintaining the establishment (this worked out at about 1s. 8d. per prisoner per day all found). Thus the life of the old, insanitary Bridewell came to an end, the building standing empty and ruinous until 1860 when it was acquired by the Venerable Archdeacon Phelps for £1,250 and after extensive rebuilding was reopened three years later as a place of public worship.

Until the establishment in 1836 of the Reading Borough Police Force, the responsibility for the maintenance of law and order within the Borough was vested in a small body of Watchmen appointed by the local Commissioners for Paving. On those rare occasions when it was possible to apprehend an offender against good order he would be lodged in some safe and reasonably secure place until such time as he could be brought before the local Bench. One of the earlier lock-ups was situated at the rear of 'The Shades' public-house (now 'La Corbiere' restaurant) in Gun Street. The use of these premises was discontinued about the time of the closure of The Oracle, a charitable establishment providing employment for the poor of the town, which was adjacent to the inn.

In later years, minor offenders against public order were lodged in a small single cell situated at the eastern end of 'Blagrave's Piazza' and known locally as 'The Hole'. The Piazza which John Mann describes as 'a most clumsy and ill formed arcade or corridor' stood against the south wall of St Lawrence's Church until demolished in 1867. Here, in a railed-off enclosure next to 'The Hole' were once stored the municipal stocks and ducking stool. The Hole and its occupants were under the care of the Head Constable who lived in The Compter House across the road. This attractive building which in addition to providing a home for the Head Constable served as Magistrates' Court until the provision in 1862 of a purpose-built Police Station and Courtroom at High Bridge House, London Street, was, it is sad to relate, destroyed in 1973 to make way for modern office development.

An anonymous diarist whose writings were published in 1877 under the title *Reading seventy years ago,* relates how four young officers of The Blues upon their regiment passing through the town amused themselves late one night by ringing doorbells and breaking knockers. In West Street they encountered the Watchman who upon challenging them was knocked to the ground. As a result of the commotion help was soon at hand and three of the young gentlemen were seized and locked in The Hole. The fourth member of the party who had succeeded in evading the Watch roused the Mayor from his bed. Sureties were arranged and the disturbers of the peace, now in more sober mood, were within the hour released on bail.

Writing in 1883, the Rev. Charles Kerry, Curate of St Lawrence's and local historian, tells with relish of the eighteenth-century Churchwarden who after a convivial evening was compelled to spend the remainder of the night in The Hole to recruit his shattered faculties before tomorrow's dawn. Thenceforward, The Hole was also spoken of as 'The churchwarden's pew'.

4 CONCERN FOR REFORM

Despite the addition in 1831 of the Juvenile Prison, the over-crowding which was first experienced following the agricultural riots did not diminish. Due to the generally unsettled state of the country and later to the establishment of local police forces the number of offenders brought before the Courts increased steadily. Regardless of the lack of prison accommodation, the Justices continued to impose prison sentences.

Within the gaol space was at a premium and all too often six or seven prisoners had to be accommodated in sleeping rooms barely adequate for more than two. Domestic and toilet facilities were severely strained and it was only with difficulty that the rudiments of discipline were maintained whilst the risk of fever was ever present. Further, in 1832 there were only 3 Turnkeys to supervise upwards of 200 prisoners. The situation must at times have had all the characteristics of a powder keg.

In their periodic reports to Quarter Sessions the Visiting Justices had little to say by way of complaint. The Chaplain, the Rev. Robert Appleton, and his successor, the Rev. John Field, were on the other hand quite outspoken in their criticism of the state of the gaol. Their concern however was less for the physical than for the spiritual well-being of the prisoners whom they felt were in danger of moral contamination. Each saw the ideal solution to the problem in the strict segregation of the prisoners one from the other. In a lengthy report to the Quarter Sessions of Michaelmas, 1841, the Rev. John Field drew the attention of the Court to the shortcomings of the regime then in force and went on to propose remedies which included an increase in the number of Turnkeys to afford constant and strict surveillance of prisoners, the appointment of a schoolmaster to impart the rudiments of education – a disturbing proportion of the inmates being illiterate – and a system of separate confinement 'to allow the criminal time for his own reflection'.

The deficiencies had not gone unnoticed by the Inspector of Prisons and in December, 1841, the Home Secretary, Sir James Graham, drew the attention of the County to the general insecurity of the prison, the facility with which male and female prisoners were able to communicate, the want of refractory cells, the insufficiency of chapel accommodation and the impossibility of the classification of the various categories of inmate according to law.

In accordance with tradition, a committee was set up to look into the matter. The 22 members were not long in arriving at their conclusion and reported to Quarter Sessions 'the present construction of the Chapel and Gaol was such as to preclude any possibility of effectual improvement'. There was no alternative, they felt, but to undertake an entire reconstruction of the whole of the interior of the prison. During the course of its deliberations the Committee consulted Col Jebb, Inspector of Prisons, who suggested that a new gaol to accommodate 150 prisoners might be erected for about £15,000. The Committee, conscious of its duty to the ratepayers, sugared the pill to some extent by suggesting that if the existing boundary walls were retained, the old materials re-used and the existing drainage system retained the reconstruction might be undertaken at much less expense.

There was in the initial stages much discussion and controversy as to the lines upon which the new gaol should operate. Should the Silent System currently in force be perpetuated or should the inmates be subject to the new 'Separate System' with its strict cellular confinement? To many the latter system appeared too soft. Hard labour and strict discipline, it was felt, was necessary if imprisonment were to have any impact. To shut the prisoner away in a cell where he would live a life of ease, said the critics, would be no punishment at all. The protagonists of the Separate System won the day and at the Easter Sessions of 1842, the Justices resolved to rebuild in a manner suited to that regime.

Whilst the debate was proceeding, the Gaol Committee inserted an advertisement in the London newspapers inviting designs for the proposed new gaol, following so far as was possible the lines of the New Model Prison at Pentonville. In order that the persons delegated to select the best design should not be tempted to show favour to any particular architect or be influenced by reputation, it was required that each competitor should submit his plans under a *nom de plume*. No fewer than seventeen entries were received, some it was later discovered prepared by architects of national repute. Several of the schemes were of great merit and the Committee faced no simple task in selecting the best. Their final decision was in respect of the design submitted by the partnership of George Gilbert Scott and Willian Bonython Moffatt, an immensely successful practice specializing in ecclesiastical buildings and public institutions whose commissions included the Home Office building in Whitehall, St Pancras Station Hotel and the Albert Memorial.

A plan prepared by a local architect, John Clacy of Friar Street, who was later to become County Architect, was considered by the Committee to be next in order of preference and was held in reserve, its author being awarded the sum of £50 for his work.

It was clear from the outset that the proposed new gaol would be of substantial construction and far from cheap to build. Could the cost be reduced? A proposal to the effect that the edifice should be reduced in scale to provide accommodation for only 150 inmates as against the architect's projected figure of 212 prisoners and 20 debtors was rejected by Quarter Sessions. It was however agreed that a saving could be effected by siting the main entrance to the north, instead of south as in the plans, thereby saving the expense of a lengthy driveway.

The amended design having been approved both by Quarter Sessions and by Col Jebb (later Sir Joshua Jebb, Surveyor-General of Prisons) under whose supervision the construction of the New Model Prison had been undertaken, tenders were invited for the clearance of the existing buildings from the site and for the erection of the new gaol. The successful applicant was the firm of John Jay, builders, of London Wall, with a tender of £24,000. Contracts were duly signed and steps taken to secure funds for the project. The money was provided by the Crown Life Assurance Co. of 33, New Bridge Street, Blackfriars, who made available to the county the sum of £24,000 at 4 per cent interest per annum secured by way of mortgage upon the County rate.

Before work could commence, arrangements had to be made to clear the gaol. This proved no easy task as there was no national organization and the prisoners could only be dispersed within the County. Fifty male and 20 female prisoners were transferred to Abingdon Gaol. Four males and two females committed from Windsor were sent back to that town to be accommodated in the local lock-up, likewise two women committed from Reading Borough Quarter Sessions were sent to the Friar Street Bridewell. The Debtors were allowed to remain and it was agreed that 52 places should be retained for prisoners committed in custody for trial.

On 18 August 1842, the builder received authority to proceed and while the surveyors commenced laying out those parts of the site which were outside the existing boundary wall, the pick-axes of the demolition workers began to bite. The first part of the old gaol to go was the Juvenile Prison. Within a month the range of buildings forming the southern part of the gaol had been levelled and the foundation trenches of the central hall and of the southern wing of the new building excavated. Soon the passer-by in Forbury Road could discern among the forest of wooden scaffolding poles and planks the gate lodge and flanking buildings taking shape.

On 11 November, activity ceased abruptly – the firm of John

Jay had failed. The Gaol Committee which met a fortnight later to consider the situation was relieved to learn that the County had suffered no financial loss on account of the bankruptcy. In accordance with the terms of the contract, the agreement with Jay was terminated and a new contract on similar terms offered to Messrs Baker & Son, builders, of Stangate Wharf, Lambeth. The new builder wasted little time in setting to work and with the coming of spring the new boundary wall with its corner turrets was complete whilst the main building was at ground-floor level. Of the old gaol there remained only the chapel and four cells in which were accommodated thirteen male debtors, one male and one female convict. Temporarily dispossessed on account of the demolition of their respective quarters, lodgings in the town were secured for the Governor, the Matron and the Storekeeper.

By June, 1843, the main building had reached the floor level of the upper storey. The outer buildings were largely complete and in order to clear away the last remnants of the old gaol which by this time housed 15 male debtors, the Chaplain's house adjoining the gate lodge was fitted up as a temporary prison. With an eye to the future, arrangements were made for the Warders to attend Pentonville Prison for instruction in the operation of the establishment under the Separate System.

The Gaol Committee was able to report to the Michaelmas Quarter Sessions that the building work was largely complete and that the east wing at least would be ready for the reception of prisoners by mid-November. The Justices were shocked, however, to learn that the cost of the work had considerably exceeded the original estimate and that the County would soon be required to foot a bill of some £40,000. The original estimate of £24,000 had already escalated to one of £33,000. Questioned closely concerning this discrepancy the Chairman explained that the architects pleaded that they had been led into error in their calculations by their surveyor.

It would seem that not only had the cost of the project been inflated by the expense of replacing the existing boundary wall, which was found to be in unsound condition, but that the architects in preparing their estimates had failed to take into account the cost of the internal fixtures and fittings. They had also omitted to include in their calculations their own fees amounting to £1,250 and the weekly sum of £3. 3s. allowed to the Clerk of Works.

A member of the Bench, the Rev. G. S. Evans, took exception on the grounds of unnecessary expense to the decorative work which adorned the exterior of the building. The Chairman of the Gaol Committee replied to the effect that whilst he, too, would have preferred a plainer style, he could state on the authority of the architect that the ornamental work added to the total cost by no more than £350.

In January, 1844, Quarter Sessions was informed that the work was progressing satisfactorily but that the prison would not be fit for occupation until the heating and ventilating apparatus had been brought into operation. This would take place in a couple of months. The cost of the work continued to escalate and the architects were obliged to request another £6,000. The project had by this time cost the County £43,648 and the Justices were thunderous in their disapproval. What earthly use was a contract if it was not adhered to, asked Mr T. Duffield MP? The Rev. Evans again criticized the ornamental work which in his view cost far more than the sum quoted by the architects – £3,500, he conceived, was nearer the mark than £350! In the view of Mr T. Goodlake, the gaol was much too large and would only be filled if there were further riots. His proposal that only part of the building be completed and that the rest be left until needed was defeated. It was agreed, not without reluctance, that there was little that could be done to rectify the situation and authority was given for further money to be borrowed in order that the work might be completed.

When the architect's accounts and bills of quantity were examined in detail it was discovered that the cost of the heating and ventilating apparatus, the kitchen equipment and the gas fittings together valued at almost £2,000 had not been taken into account.

Some additional expense was unavoidable. The unstable nature of the soil near the Kennet demanded deeper foundations for the south-west turret than had been anticipated, whilst the original boundary wall which was to have been retained was found to be in such poor condition that there was no alternative but to rebuild at a cost of £3,250. Additional expense was also incurred through departures from the original plan suggested by the architect and approved by the Gaol Committee – the provision of 16 additional cells in the main building (£800), an additional storey to the female wing providing 5 extra cells (£600), the erection of the pump house (£200) and the provision of sub-basements in the main building and female wing to accommodate the boilers and heating apparatus (£590).

By Easter, the Gaol committee was able to report that the main building was complete and that the women's prison was in the final stages of fitting out. Unfortunately it was not yet possible for the gaol to accept prisoners as the brickwork was not sufficiently dry. It was promised, nevertheless, that all would be in readiness by Midsummer. The builders were as good as their word and at the Midsummer Sessions held on 1 July, 1844, the gaol was declared fit to receive 185 male prisoners and the premises were formally handed over to the County.

During the months prior to the completion of the building work, the Gaol Committee had been very busy. Tenders for the supply of goods and services were invited and carefully examined, contracts being awarded to the tradespeople offering terms most advantageous to the County. Among the tenders sought was that for the supply of gas to the premises. The Reading Gas Light Co., suppliers to the old gaol, offered gas at a cost of 7s. per 1,000 cubic feet. Their rival, The Reading Union Gas Co., tendered 6s. 10d. per 1,000 cubic feet and it was accordingly proposed that the lower tender be accepted. The matter was on the point of being put to the vote when it was pointed out that the Reading Gas Light Co. had already laid the necessary mains and pipes and that, furthermore, the Company had agreed to maintain these free of charge. This consideration was felt to outweigh the cheaper rate of The Union Gas Co. and for once the higher tender was accepted.

The question of staffing the new gaol was debated at length. It was beyond dispute that the establishment of the old gaol was completely inadequate but how large a staff would be needed? After much argument it was agreed that the existing members of staff be confirmed in post and that their numbers be augmented by the appointment of four assistant warders at an annual salary of £30, an engineer (£52), a cook (£30), a porter (£30) and a prison servant, a kind of caretaker–handyman (£20). To make the position more attractive it was agreed that all employees with the exception of the Governor, the Chaplain and the Surgeon, receive in addition to their wage a daily ration of bread (1 lb.), meat (1 lb.), potatoes (1 lb.), coffee ($\frac{3}{4}$ oz.), sugar (2 oz.) and milk ($\frac{1}{2}$ pt.). They were also to receive $\frac{1}{2}$ lb. of fresh butter weekly together with 'a sufficiency of pepper, salt, mustard, vinegar and onions'.

The daily routine for both staff and inmates was laid down in detail as was the scale of dietary. Whilst the building was modelled on that at Pentonville, it was readily apparent that the regime of a county gaol could never follow that of an establishment intended to prepare prisoners for Transportation. The New Model Prison catered for young men blessed with reasonable health and physique who were to spend a minimum of eighteen months there before leaving the country. Reading Gaol, on the other hand, would be obliged to accept prisoners of both sexes, of all ages, conditions and habits for varying periods – a few days, a few weeks but only rarely for more than a few months. It would not under these circumstances be practicable to afford training in manufacturing crafts such as wood-turning or weaving as this would involve much expense with little return, if any. The new prison must be reformative in its deterrence. In the words of the Chairman of the Gaol Committee:

The old and hardened prisoner will no longer find in the Wards of his prison a sort of clubroom but little irksome to him on account of the fellowship of many like himself and what is of far higher importance, the casual offender simple and ignorant perhaps rather than vicious will be saved from the infection of evil companionship even should instruction fail to produce the customary fruits.

It was hoped that in the majority of cases of offenders committed to Reading Gaol, the minimum period of imprisonment prescribed by law for their respective crimes should prove ample punishment.

County business having been transacted, the Quarter Sessions proceeded to work through the criminal calendar. The first person to be tried and sentenced to a term of imprisonment with hard labour in the new Gaol was one Abraham Boswell of Waltham St Lawrence, indicted of offences of indecent assault and attempted rape against a child aged 2 years. The sentence – 6 months imprisonment with hard labour.

By Michaelmas of 1844 the gaol under the Governorship of Edward Hackett was operating smoothly and efficiently. Word had indeed spread throughout the County that Reading Gaol was not to be recommended and there was a noticeable decline in the number of persons before the Courts for serious crime. In their quarterly report to Quarter Sessions the Visiting Justices commented that 'the prisoners answer thankfully they have no complaint to make'. The Chaplain in his report is far more realistic in his observation that 'the separation of the criminals is irksome to many (or to use their own expressive term "very wicked")'.

The builders, it was generally agreed, had done their work well and few modifications were required. The one major defect concerned the laundry room in the basement of the female wing. The need for efficient ventilation does not appear to have been taken into account and when the coppers were lighted the temperature here was so high and the atmosphere so steamy as to be unbearable. The bad conditions could not be remedied and an external laundry was erected near the women's exercise yard and the original room adapted for use as an infirmary. In the main building, leaking water tanks caused considerable nuisance in the early stages. The Reading water, it seems, had a corrosive effect upon the lead which, at a cost of £60, was replaced by cast iron after which all was well.

During the first year of its operation the new gaol was visited by representatives of the Justices of Buckinghamshire, Northamptonshire and Warwickshire, all of whom appeared favourably impressed and expressed considerable interest in the new system of management. The Magistrates of Berkshire, after their earlier misgivings, were highly delighted and commented:

> The new system of discipline has now been in operation a year and the results it presents are calculated to afford the deepest and most serious satisfaction to the Court and the County at large . . . we are justified in stating that at least a majority of those who have been a reasonable time under the discipline at Reading Gaol will leave it with the firm resolution to obtain henceforth an honest livelihood.

The metamorphosis was complete.

5 THE NEW COUNTY GAOL

Standing, as it does, on the rising ground at the
entrance to Reading, and close to the site of the
venerable abbey, this new prison is from every side
the most conspicuous building, and, architecturally,
by far the greatest ornament to the town.

– The *Illustrated London News*,
17 February, 1844

The largest of the town's public buildings, the new gaol built
of red Tilehurst brick with decorative quoins of Bath stone, the
turrets and crenellations creating the impression of a fifteenth-
century castle, was indeed imposing.

The whole site was enclosed by a boundary wall of smooth
brickwork some 18 ft in height. At each corner were turrets
serving as living quarters for members of the staff. That at the
north-west corner was reserved for the Deputy Governor. That
at the north-eastern angle and integral with the women's wing
was occupied by the Matron, whose only means of access to her
quarters was through the main hall of that building. The remaining turrets being of a more modest pattern offered accommodation for 2 married Warders and their families. These latter
quarters with their octagonal rooms and spiral staircases were
cramped and inconvenient. Comfort was however secondary to
security, the buildings being so designed that their grated windows commanded a clear view of the flanking walls both internally and externally, thus facilitating the detection of any attempt
to scale the walls from within, or to aid any such attempt from
without.

The Governor and the Chaplain each occupied a four-bedroomed house of generous proportions either side of the main gate. At basement level, in addition to the kitchen, scullery and pantry, were separate cellars for beer and wine. On the ground floor were situated dining- and drawing-rooms and for the Chaplain, a study. The Governor's house was provided with a small office with access to the prison courtyard. On the two upper floors were the bedrooms, bathroom and dressing-room.

Outside the boundary wall to the east of the prison were stables, a shed for the prison caravan and a separate house for the Governor's gig. This area was under the charge of the Warder–Coachman who occupied a bothy above the stables. Adjoining the stable block was the Guard Room of the Berkshire Militia and the entrance to a covered way leading to the military stores and armoury situated beneath the east wing of the prison. This entrance did not permit access to any other part of the building or grounds and did not come within the jurisdiction of the prison authorities.

The only entrance to the prison was by way of the main gate to the north of the site. The heavy iron-studded wooden gates were set between two small turrets, the narrow loopholed windows of which were arranged to permit enfilading fire to be brought to bear in case of attack. The flat roof with its battlements was also designed to provide a vantage point for riflemen in times of emergency. Behind the parapet were machiolations allowing the defenders on the roof a clear view of any assailant sufficiently bold to approach the gates below. The flat roof was intended also to provide a stage upon which public executions might be carried out. The ground floor of the western turret served as a gatekeeper's lodge; opposite was a waiting room. In the rooms above the gate was accommodation for 3 unmarried Warders.

Within the gates was a paved courtyard across which was the entrance to the main building. To the left was the doorway of the female wing.

The main building was in the form of a cross, the four wings radiating from a lofty, domed central hall beneath the tower. This area was the hub of the prison. Here the staff upon reporting for duty would assemble for inspection and to receive their orders. On the ground floor was the Governor's office. At first floor level was the office of the Deputy Governor with its glazed inspection gallery affording a clear view of the interior of the building. Across the hall was the Committee Room and another room of similar dimensions in which the Visiting Justices assembled to receive applications by the prisoners and to deal with disciplinary matters.

With the exception of the Debtors, the prisoners were housed in the wings extending to the east, south and west. These were of three storeys. At ground-floor level the cells opened on to a central corridor some 15 ft in width, open to the vaulted roof. On the floors above, the cells opened on to railed galleries 3 ft in width supported on wall brackets. At first floor level, wire netting was stretched across the well to check the fall of anyone who by accident or design were to drop over the railings.

The east and west wings were 120 ft in length with 25 cells to each gallery, the south wing much shorter with only 12 cells at each level. For administrative convenience, the wings were referred to as A, B and C respectively; the galleries were numbered 1, 2 and 3 whilst the cells were numbered from 1 upwards. Each cell could in this way be readily identified. By way of example, cell No. 6 on the second gallery in the east wing would be known as 'A2.6'. It was the custom in the nineteenth century to refer to each prisoner by his cell location rather than by name and each wore on his jacket a badge bearing that reference. During his period at Reading, Oscar Wilde's location and personal reference was C3.3.

The cell in which each prisoner was required to live and work measured 13 ft × 7 ft × 10 ft in height. The floors were of red and black tiles, the walls of whitewashed brick. The doors of the cells were of heavy wood, studded with iron. The lock which was strong and heavy was inaccessible from within in order that it should not be picked or jammed. A small glass-covered peep hole with a moveable shutter allowed the occupant to be observed without his being aware of the fact. Below was a lockable trap through which food and work materials might be passed. Light was admitted through two small vertical windows each of eight small panes glazed with clear glass, set high in the wall. Artificial lighting was by coal gas. For safety's sake there could be no gas piping in the cell. The burner with its incandescent mantle was placed in a 'gas box', an aperture of approximately 9 in. × 9 in. in the corridor wall with a glazed opening through which the light could shine into the cell.

Each cell was provided with a small copper washhand-basin and an earthenware W.C., facilities sadly lacking in even the most modern of prison buildings. The prisoner was permitted a daily allowance of water which was metered in a simple but effective manner. Along each gallery ran a square iron pipe divided internally into sections of 6 gallons capacity, one to each cell. Each morning, water was admitted to the trough until all the sections were filled. The turncock was then closed leaving each prisoner with his ration to use as he thought fit.

The prisoner was deprived of all personal belongings and the items officially issued to him were few in number, the principal being a tin plate, two mugs, a spoon, cleaning materials and brushes. Cell furnishings were of the simplest – a three-legged stool, a fixed table and a set of shelves. Until the introduction later in the century of the plank bed, each prisoner slept in a hammock which he slung from hooks set in the side walls of the cell. By day, the hammock and bedding after airing were neatly rolled and placed on one of the shelves.

Communication between the prisoner and the Warder was effected by means of a gong operated from within the cell by a pull handle. Upon the gong being sounded, a trip device outside the cell door would cause a small signal arm to drop enabling the Warder readily to observe the cell from which the summons came. It was, of course, a strict rule that the Warder should be summoned only in case of emergency and the penalty for abuse was severe.

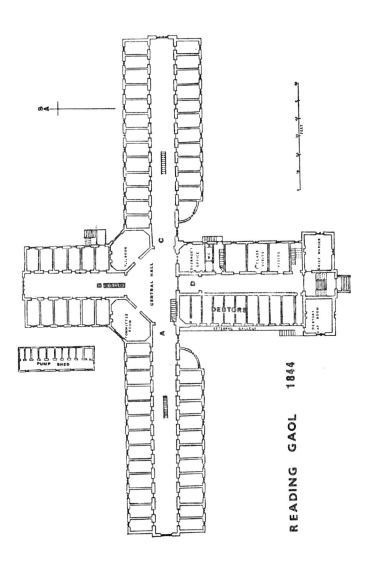

READING GAOL 1844

The principal entrance to the building was by the main door which opened on to a flight of steps leading into the north or D Wing. Through the centre of this wing was a corridor which led to a pair of glazed doors giving access to the central hall. On the right-hand side of this passageway were the Head Warder's room, a visiting room in which the prisoner and his visitors sat in wire mesh enclosed compartments with a Warder between, a less austere room in which solicitors and other privileged persons might interview their prisoner clients, and at the farther end, the Governor's office. Adjoining the Governor's office was a lobby with toilet facilities, a private entrance and a private staircase to the chapel on the floor above.

On the opposite side was a day room and ten 'sleeping rooms' for the First Class Debtors. These cells were unusual in that there was no ready communication with the body of the prison. The sleeping rooms which were of similar dimensions to the normal cells opened directly on to an external gallery leading to the day room, an arrangement which must have been extremely uncomfortable in bad weather. Below, separated by a high wall from the grounds surrounding the prison was the Debtor's airing yard.

The gentle slope of the site permitted the construction of a basement area beneath A, B and D Wings. One half of the basement of A Wing was designated the County Stores and was employed as an armoury and equipment store by the Berkshire Militia; there was no access other than by way of the covered passage to the guard room already described. The remainder of A Wing basement was occupied by the kitchen. Installed by Messrs Haden, the coppers and steamers were heated by steam from the boilers in the sub-basement. These coke-fired boilers not only supplied steam to the kitchen but also powered the heating and ventilating apparatus. The system designed and constructed by George and James Haden of Trowbridge had already proved highly successful at the New Model Prison. The whole building was warmed by fresh air which, having been passed over an iron case heated by very hot water, was conducted to the cells through ducts built into the fabric of the walls. In this way an even temperature was maintained. A further advantage was that the prisoners were unable to communicate by 'pipe tapping' as would have been the case had conventional hot water pipes been installed. The stale air was extracted from the building through the central ventilating tower.

Beneath D Wing were the reception cells in which prisoners newly received from Court were lodged until the formalities connected with their committal had been completed. Here, too, were facilities for fumigating, cleansing and storing prisoners' property. In this area, situated beneath the First Class Debtors' accommodation was a day room and cells for the Second Class Debtors, persons committed for contempt of Court through peculation. Debtors of this class were denied many of the privileges afforded to those sent to prison on account of their inability to meet their debts.

Beneath the Central Hall were store rooms and the Warders' mess.

Beneath B Wing were the baths. Near by were the dark cells in which offenders against discipline could be ordered to be detained in solitary confinement. These cells were provided with neither window nor artificial lighting and were fitted with double doors to render them soundproof. It was customary for the new arrival to be shown these dungeons to impress upon him the fate which awaited the uncooperative.

On the upper floor of D Wing was the chapel. Measuring 55 ft × 42 ft the interior resembled less a church than a large lecture theatre. There was accommodation for a congregation of 192, each prisoner occupying a single cubicle from which he could see none of his fellows yet himself be under the observation of Warders strategically placed in a gallery above the Chancel. The cubicles were too narrow to permit the occupant to kneel whilst the seats were in effect only a sloping ledge against which he could rest when not required to stand. A chapel of similar design is preserved in the old gaol, now the County Records Office, at Lincoln. It was not until 1873 that flat seats upon which one could sit in comfort were introduced. The female prisoners sat in the well of the chapel screened from the gaze of the males by a curtain. They entered by a staircase from the corridor below. The male prisoners entered by two doorways leading from the upper gallery of the central hall. Situated between these doorways was the organ loft. The chapel could be filled and emptied in minutes without undue haste, a procedure aided by a semaphore instrument operated by the Warder in charge indicating the order in which the pews were to be vacated.

At the front of the building and on the same level as the chapel was the male infirmary comprising two convalescent rooms measuring 20 ft × 15 ft with the Surgeon's room and dispensary above.

Under the Separate System, the only time that a prisoner left his cell was to attend chapel or to take his exercise. The daily exercise period was a model of rigid planning, the inmates being taken from their cells in predetermined order and making their way fifteen paces apart to a structure situated in the south-west corner of the grounds. Seen from above the exercise yard resembled a huge cartwheel with twenty spokes each 40 ft in length. Each spoke was in reality a wall behind which a prisoner marched up and down for the requisite period. No prisoner could see or communicate with any other yet all were under the constant observation of a Warder posted in a circular pillbox forming the hub of the wheel.

The female prisoners were strictly segregated from the males and were accommodated in a separate wing (E Wing) situated to the east of the main gate. There were 31 cells in 3 galleries, the windows overlooking the yard. There were no windows or openings in the north wall which formed part of the boundary. In the basement were situated two dark cells for refractory prisoners, baths, a small infirmary in the area originally intended as the laundry and a small room for the occasional female debtor.

This wing had its own exercise yard of six walled walks each

40 ft in length by 10 ft in width. Observation was kept from a narrow passageway provided with a window opening upon each run.

It was the intention of the architects that the area surrounding the prison should be as little encumbered as possible in order that the staff might have a clear view of the grounds and that opportunities for a prisoner to secrete himself might be strictly limited. Other than the exercise yards and laundry the only other building was the pump shed, a structure measuring 45 ft $\times$ 12 ft situated in the angle between A and B Wings. Here, 10 prisoners, each in his separate compartment, operated the hand-crank by means of which water for use in the prison was pumped to an overhead cistern.

From about 1844 the number of persons committed to prison from the Courts of the county began steadily to decrease. From over one thousand in 1844, the registers showed a drop in admissions to 805 in 1847. Three years later, in 1850, the annual intake had fallen to a mere 637. It would be easy to suppose that news of the regime of solitary confinement had spread around the county and that would-be wrongdoers were suitably deterred and had mended their ways. There were in truth more complicated factors both social and economic bearing upon the situation, but the Justices nevertheless congratulated themselves upon their wisdom and foresight in adopting the 'Separate System'. On the other hand, those who had earlier criticized the new building on account of its size began to feel that their warnings were not in vain. During the early months of 1847 there were fewer than 80 prisoners accommodated in an establishment intended for over 200. Help was however to come from the Government. In 1841, Pentonville Prison was established with a view to accepting prisoners sentenced to Transportation for a period of preparation for the new life that they were to lead in Van Dieman's Land. The 'training' took place under conditions of silence and segregation. Upon the completion of eighteen months at Pentonville the prisoner, according to his behaviour, industry and moral outlook was allocated to one of three classes:

'Ticket of Leave' (first class), 'Probation Pass' (second class) or 'Probation Gang' (third class). A 'Ticket of Leave' man would be allowed to land in certain parts of Australia with a free pardon conditional upon his undertaking not to return to the United Kingdom until his sentence had expired. It was natural therefore that the majority of such prisoners would make determined efforts to attain First Class status ('completely reformed'). From this point of view the Pentonville system was a success and the Inspectors looked about for other prisons in which this process could be undertaken. The empty cells at Reading, which was by design a miniature Pentonville, provided a ready solution and an approach was accordingly made to Quarter Sessions. After negotiation it was agreed that 40 cells should be made available at a rental of £6 per cell per year. In order that the existing staff should not be overburdened by the task of supervising the 'Government Convicts' it was further agreed that two Assistant Warders, an Assistant Schoolmaster and a Trades Instructor be engaged at Government expense. The salaries of the Governor, Deputy Governor and Chaplain were raised by £50 per year whilst the Surgeon was granted an additional £20.

The contract was signed at the Midsummer Sessions and on 5 August the first batch of 40 convicts arrived from Millbank Penitentiary for their period of 'religious and moral training'. The Visiting Justices in their report to Michaelmas Sessions (October 1847) say that many of the men arrived 'with minds unsettled and unfavourable to discipline either denying their guilt or expecting to receive pardons'. Of one of the more difficult prisoners it is reported that 'predetermined to "run cranky" he feigned insanity from which he was promptly recovered by the application of a lunatic waistcoat and gloves. It has since been necessary to flog him for mutinous conduct and he is now well behaved'. The Rev. Field took his responsibilities seriously and reports with pride that 'one Transport has in two months committed to memory the four Gospels'.

The termination of the contract came under consideration in

1848, a year of famine and unrest, when the gaol was called upon to receive an unprecedented number of persons of both sexes sent to prison for vagrancy and workhouse offences and every available cell was required for them. In January of that year there were no fewer than 181 prisoners in custody, by April there were 204 and it was necessary to transfer many of them to Abingdon. With the coming of summer the vagrants had served their sentences and moved on. There were empty cells again in plenty and the county felt justified in adhering to the contract. Government convicts continued to be accommodated here until May, 1856, by which time the sentence of Penal Servitude had replaced that of Transportation. The departure of the Government prisoners was regarded with dismay by the staff as Quarter Sessions, with its eye as always upon economy, resolved immediately to restore the establishment and salaries to the scale obtaining at the date of the signing of the contract. The salaries of the Governor and Chaplain were reduced by £50 a year whilst the Deputy Governor was mulcted of £20. With rare generosity the Justices allowed the pay of the Surgeon (£100) and of the Clerk (£30) to remain unchanged. The Assistant Schoolmaster having resigned through ill health and the Trades Instructor having been dismissed for misconduct, their places were allowed to remain vacant. The two Assistant Warders were retained, a Committee of Justices appointed to look into the question of staffing being of the opinion that the setting up of a County Police Force was almost certain to bring about an increase in the number of convictions for criminal offences and consequent committals to prison.

The preoccupation of the prison authorities with religious instruction as a means of social rehabilitation has already been mentioned. The insistence of the Visiting Justices, indeed of the whole body of County Justices, upon the prisoners being compelled to undertake a course of quite intense religious study was criticized in 1850 by Capt. Williams, Inspector of Prisons, in his annual report. The substance of his remarks was that in Reading Gaol neither labour nor employment was provided for the prisoners as required by law and that they were thrown on the simple resource of learning by heart whole chapters or even Books of the Scriptures which in many instances they did not even understand.

In an angry protest to the Home Secretary, the Visiting Justices expressed the opinion that Capt. Williams's visits to the gaol did not amount in hours to the number of years that the establishment had been in operation and that the employment which was provided for the inmates was such as to lead them to ask a favour for the work that the Inspector considered such an imposition.

The question of religious instruction and how it might be afforded most effectively could stir the deepest passions. In the Summer of 1850 a disagreement between the Chaplain and the Visiting Justices over the style of Bible to be used by the prisoners caused tempers to run high. To assist the prisoners in the preparation of written exercises which were marked on a weekly basis by the Chaplain, the Rev. Field introduced Bibles with marginal notes. This innovation angered the Visiting Justices who, having failed to persuade the Chaplain to withdraw the annotated Bibles and to restore the plain variety which had been in use from 1844, complained to the Lord Bishop of the Diocese. The Chaplain for his part saw this as an interference with his office and continued as before turning a deaf ear both to the remonstrances of the Visiting Justices and of the Bishop. The Justices expressed the view that the use of the annotated Bible relieved the prisoner of the necessity to read his Scripture, to research and to exercise thought – all he needed to complete the exercises was to copy the notes. Of greater significance was their feeling that the Rev. Field was taking to himself 'uncontrolled power to alter, to omit or to continue at any time any part of the daily instruction'. The Justices were jealous of their authority and would permit no one to encroach upon it.

In order to bring the Chaplain into conformity it was proposed at the next meeting of Quarter Sessions that the Prison Rules should be formally amended to provide that all prisoners should attend Divine Service daily, that they should receive regular instruction by the Chaplain and further, 'Prisoners shall be taught to read and write and learn by heart portions of the Holy Scripture and that exercises which have been made weekly by the Prisoners shall be prepared with the assistance only of Bibles having no marginal references; and after inspection by the Chaplain shall be fairly written in copy books.'

The proposed rule could not be brought into effect without the prior approval of the Home Secretary and the matter was accordingly referred to Whitehall for attention. The dispute continued to smoulder with the Chaplain unwilling to conform to the demands of the Justices. The Justices for their part were equally uncompromising. No word having been received from the Home Office as to the proposed rule relating to religious instruction, in November 1850 the Visiting Justices lodged a formal complaint with the Home Secretary concerning the Chaplain's conduct. To add weight they went on to add that the Rev. Field when preparing his publication *The Life of Howard* illegally employed convicts under sentence of Transportation to copy out his manuscript. He had in truth quite openly arranged for a former Cambridge undergraduate, Bellamy, to assist him in correcting the proofs. The Chaplain admitted that Bellamy was thus engaged for a short time only. The Visiting Justices claimed that he was working for the Chaplain from mid-January until mid-April.

In his reply to the Visiting Justices, the Home Secretary, Sir George Grey, skilfully evaded too deep an involvement in the issue and expressed the view that the differences between the Chaplain and the Visiting Justices could surely be adjusted without the influence of higher authority. With regard to the Chaplain's unauthorized employment of a prisoner to copy his proofs, he mentioned that the matter had already been noticed by the Inspector who had pointed out the impropriety of such a course. Nothing was said concerning the proposed rule and in time better counsel prevailed.

By 1851 the hitherto inflexible attitude of the Justices as to the form of training best suited to the prisoners began to change with consideration being given to the means whereby the sentence of imprisonment with hard labour might more realistically be put into effect. At long last the detrimental effects of solitary confinement for long periods was taken into account and a Committee appointed to look into the matter. The Committee remarking upon the 'relaxed state of muscular power and a diminution of physical energy' in prisoners serving all but the shortest of sentences was unanimous in its opinion that some form of hard physical labour ought to be provided. Whilst it was not proposed that the treadmill should be reintroduced into the prison, it was nevertheless suggested that a mill for grinding flour 'open to the atmospheric air' would not only afford the prisoners employment but would effect a saving and compensate in great measure for the outlay involved. Two suggestions were made: the erection of a building similar to the pump house in which was milling machinery suitable for operation by 40 prisoners turning a hand crank. The cost together with bakehouse and oven was estimated at £700. For an outlay of about £400 it was suggested that the same number of prisoners could be employed in the operation of hand mills in their own cells. The former proposal was preferred in that it would provide the opportunity for exercise and fresh air but in view of the cost and because measures were shortly to be laid before Parliament for the reduction of the County Rate the Committee felt it inexpedient to make any strong recommendation at that stage.

The Chaplain for his part viewed the changing attitude of the Justices with grave misgiving and in his annual report deplored the suggestion that there should be any relaxation in the policy of separation. Religious instruction, he insisted, was the only sure means of preventing crime adding, 'When it is remembered that these men are under sentence for atrocious offences committed in most cases after previous conviction and a life of profligacy and crime it is unreasonable to look for permanent

correction as the result of imprisonment so comparatively short.'
It would seem that in the eyes of the Rev. Field, not only were
sentences too short but also that the prisoners' working day was
insufficiently long. Complaining that the hour of retiring should
be at 9 p.m. instead of at 8, he goes on to say that even then the
men would be allowed an hour more in sleep than was really
necessary.

By Government decree in 1854, the period of separate confinement was limited to nine months, after which time the
prisoner should be engaged in associated labour. A further
recommendation was made by the Visiting Justices to Quarter
Sessions that some form of heavy manual labour should be
devised preferably the grinding of corn to produce flour for use
in the prison. Quarter Sessions agreed and by the end of the
year three hand mills were placed on order. A baker's oven was
installed and a Miller and Baker engaged at a weekly wage of
18s.

A sample hand mill, a machine resembling a very large
domestic mincer, was tested and found satisfactory in all respects
except that it was capable of grinding and dressing only one
bushel of grain in a working day of $5\frac{1}{2}$ hours. Six mills were
accordingly ordered. The order having been placed there was
a delay of nearly a year before the machines were received, the
manufacturers explaining that such was the demand for their
apparatus they could not hope to satisfy all their customers
immediately. By the Autumn of 1855 the mills were at last in
operation and the prison again supplied with 'coarse but
wholesome' bread baked from flour made on the premises.

The scope of hard labour was extended in 1863 by the introduction of stonebreaking. For this purpose no apparatus other
than hammers and shovels was required. Rough granite and
flint could be purchased at reasonable prices and there was a
demand for the broken stone for use as roadmetal. The airing
yard adjacent to the women's wing was cleared and a stoneyard
set up in its place. The project was not as profitable as the
Justices had hoped, indeed there was a deficit of £10 at the end

of the first year of operation. It was however decided that the form of labour which was both exhausting and monotonous was so effective a means of keeping the prisoners occupied that the loss could be justified.

By 1870, the value of photography as a ready means of identification of criminals was recognized and the Commissioner of Police of the Metropolis requested that photographs of persistent criminals should be made available to him. It was also appreciated that a photograph could be of inestimable value not only in the event of an escape but also on those not infrequent occasions when a prisoner was suspected of having served a previous sentence under a different name. The Governor was accordingly sent to look into the system of photographing prisoners that had recently been introduced to Winchester Prison. In due course a contract was made with Mr Thomas Wood, photographer of 67, Broad Street, for full and side face photographs of the prisoners at a cost of 1s. 9d. per pair. Photography was at first undertaken out of doors. This was not a particularly satisfactory arrangement and a small studio was erected near the exercise yard. This venture into modern technology was not however long lived as after six months during which time there were no escapes nor cases of suspected impersonation the Visiting Justices expressed the view that the expense was out of all proportion to the value and the contract was rescinded. The Visiting Justices, one feels, were greatly influenced in their decision by the refusal of the Commissioner of Police to meet the cost of the photographs of recidivists which had been made available to him.

Public execution of criminals being no longer legal, the little studio was converted into an execution chamber. In the centre of the floor a brick-lined pit was excavated measuring 9 ft by 5 ft by 8 ft in depth. The mouth of the pit was closed by a pair of trap doors secured on the underside by three iron bars. One end hinged, the other secured by a lever-operated locking device, the bars when released would drop allowing the trap doors to fall open. Above the drop, supported by two uprights was a stout wooden beam to which the rope would be fastened. This gallows was first employed in March, 1877, for the double execution of the brothers Francis and Henry Tidbury. On that occasion the shed must have been crowded to capacity as not only were prison officials in attendance but invitations were also extended to Justices of the Peace and to representatives of the Press. One person who chose not to be present was the Chaplain, the Rev. Maurice Friend, for whom a pane of glass was removed in order that he might intone from outside suitable prayers in the hearing of the condemned. This building remained in use until the turn of the century when the First Class Debtors' cells in D Wing were converted into a self-contained suite of two enlarged cells each with its own bathroom and toilet. Between the two condemned cells was a passageway leading to the drop which was installed in a wooden structure projecting from the side of the building. The drop was demolished in 1968 and the condemned cells converted into offices.

With the passing of the Prisons Act of 1877, the ownership of the site and buildings was transferred to the Crown for a consideration of £6,066. 5s. In many counties the assumption by the central Government of rights and powers which had been the prerogative of the Justices of the Peace for some 500 years was strongly resisted. The Berkshire Justices, with a keen eye to the County purse, approved generally of the measure but nevertheless expressed the view that the most effective constant supervision could only be secured through the continuance of the system of Visiting Justices. The Home Secretary was able to meet the Justices half-way by authorizing the establishment of Visiting Committees of Justices, the role of which is outlined in chapter 1 of this book.

The preliminaries to the transfer of responsibility for management involved the Governor and the Clerk in a flood of administrative work. The County required that all stocks of prison produce and raw material should be sold and the proceeds credited to the County Treasurer, existing contracts for the supply of goods were to be terminated and inventories and returns correct in the minutest detail were to be compiled. One of the last orders of Quarter Sessions before the transfer was to award a gratuity of £20, a handsome sum, to the Clerk in recognition of his services at this time. An indication of the strain to which he must have been subject can be seen in an error by which he allowed a prisoner to be discharged seven days before the expiration of his sentence. For this unprecedented lapse the unfortunate Clerk was severely reprimanded.

Unlike a great many of the prisons which were taken over by the Government, Reading was both efficient in operation and structurally in first-class condition. Not long since had the patent asphalte roofs been replaced with lead, the drainage system, which had hitherto discharged directly into the Kennet, connected to the town sewers and the water piping almost completely replaced. Indeed the only work that was required was the removal of the covered way between the Militia Store, now vacated, and the guard room in Forbury Road. This gateway was securely bricked up as was the entrance to the basement of A Wing.

It would be tedious to catalogue the minor alterations which have from time to time been carried out within the building. A prison, like any large institution, is a living community in which changes must of necessity take place from time to time and adaptations need be made. Within the main building the most obvious change was seen in the chapel from which the tiered floor and box pews were removed in 1879. The large room which once served as the First Class Debtors' day-room was appointed the Roman Catholic chapel. On the south side of A Wing two cells were adapted for the accommodation of prisoners suffering from tuberculosis whilst in C Wing a padded cell for the violently insane was installed. Externally, outbuildings for use as workshops and stores were built as required while the wagon-wheel pattern exercise yards were demolished to make way for the circular walk in which the prisoners could take the air together.

With the exception of a small brick built studio nestling

between A and D Wings, erected in 1884 when the photography of prisoners was resumed, the majority of the outbuildings were swept away in the rebuilding programme which commenced in 1968 and is now nearing completion, being replaced by the modern workshop block. Of this development more will be told in a later chapter.

6 PRISON LIFE

Prior to the nineteenth century the primary task of the Keeper of the County Gaol was to hold safely and securely those persons who had been committed to his care until such time as they were required to stand trial or were otherwise dealt with according to law. Security was his concern – punishment or reformation did not enter into his calculations. Rudimentary rules were indeed laid down for the conduct of the gaol and for the preservation of good order (see Chapter 11) but these do not seem to have been enforced with any great rigidity until late in the eighteenth century. What did it matter, argued the Keeper, if the prisoners had a little enjoyment? If they were happy they were less likely to attempt to escape or to rebel, and what better way of keeping them happy than making available plenty of strong drink? The general public were not always in agreement and as early as March, 1661, we find two burgesses of Reading complaining to the Mayor and Corporation 'that there is great disorders in the gaol by reason of the Gaoler's keeping a common alehouse there'. It was accordingly resolved that representations be made to the Justices of the county at the next Sessions for some action to be taken to mitigate the nuisance. The protest appears to have had remarkably little effect as the sale of liquor within the prison persisted for some 150 years.

In those early days a prisoner with money enjoyed a decided advantage in that he could obtain for himself not only extra food and drink but other privileges such as extra bedding and even lighter chains and manacles. Living conditions both at the County Gaol in Castle Street and at the Town Bridewell in Friar Street were nevertheless far from attractive as witnessed by the accounts of John Howard and John Man. There was little or no privacy. There was no segregation of the sexes except for sleeping quarters, neither was there separate accommodation for untried prisoners or for juveniles. Violence, noise and squalor were ever in evidence.

With the transfer of the gaol to the Forbury it was possible to introduce a more structured system and to this end a comprehensive set of rules relating to the conduct of both staff and inmates was drawn up in 1792 and submitted to Quarter Sessions for approval in readiness for the move.

For the first time rules were made which allowed the Justices a considerable degree of control over the way in which their employees behaved towards the prisoners. The Keeper (he was not designated Governor until 1840) was required to enter into a bond of £100 which would be forfeit to Quarter Sessions in the event of any misconduct on his part. Any negligence on his part which contributed to the escape of a prisoner could also be visited by the loss of his bond. It was further ordered that the two Turnkeys should be paid six months in arrears in order that the County might have a firm control over them the reasoning being that, whereas a man might be prepared to run the risk of dismissal should he embark upon a course of disobedience, he would certainly think twice if half a year's pay were at stake. Indeed, any major breach of discipline could result not only in the termination of his services but in the loss of the wages retained in hand. As the Turnkeys were quartered in the gaol on an 'all found' basis, it would seem that the authorities were of the opinion that they had no real need for money. Opportunities to spend their money were few as they were not allowed to leave the premises without the prior permission of the Keeper and even then had to be back not later than 10 p.m.

The rules relating to the conduct of the prison staff were quite explicit. The Keeper was required in the execution of his duties 'to guard against every impulse of anger or personal resentment'. He was not to strike any prisoner except in self-defence neither was he 'to hold any unnecessary conversation with his prisoners' but was to give his commands and to attend to their needs in as few words as possible. The Turnkeys were enjoined neither to swear, to curse, be drunk nor to strike any prisoner except in self-defence or in the protection of the Keeper.

The Keeper and his subordinate officers were required to work cruelly long hours with very little free time. A working day of 14 to 15 hours was not unusual. The staff were required to live on the premises and married men who applied for employment as Turnkeys were warned that there was no provision for the accommodation of their families and that they would receive no concession on account of their status of husband or father.

For the prisoners, living conditions in the rebuilt gaol were greatly superior to those experienced in the establishment in Castle Street. It was intended that not only would each category of prisoner be segregated but that each inmate would have his own cell in which to sleep and be provided with his own bed complete with chaff-filled mattress, blanket, rug and sheet of hemp or coarse linen. Unhappily, as the prison population increased, this was no longer possible and by 1825, the Keeper was obliged to accommodate the prisoners three to a cell.

To make escape less easy the prisoners were originally required to wear the blue and yellow dress noted by John Man in his account of 1810. This bizarre garb gave way in 1828 to a more serviceable and long-wearing outfit of jacket, waistcoat and trousers in brown fustian. The prisoners were also supplied with knitted woollen underwear, socks and a striped cotton shirt. The garments came in two sizes only – boys' and men's. One suspects that the authorities worked on the assumption that it was easier to put a small man into a large suit than *vice versa*. With the exception of the knitted items this clothing was purchased from local suppliers. In 1876, the contract was awarded to Messrs Heelas of Broad Street for men's suits at 17s. 10d., boys' at 13s. 9d. An additional item of prison clothing which came into use with the adoption of the 'Separate System' was a cloth cap with an elongated peak which, when pulled down over the face, formed a kind of mask. It was a strict rule that when prisoners were together the peak or 'beak' was to be lowered in order that one might not recognize the other.

The diet was not particularly imaginative. During the early years of the nineteenth century the daily allowance of food, the cost of which was met from County funds, was a mere 1½ lb. of bread with water. Vegetables from the garden were occasionally served on weekdays whilst on Sundays there might be a small portion of meat. This meagre diet was revised in 1825 in accordance with a rule to the effect that each prisoner should receive 'sufficient quantity of bread and water and other coarse but wholesome food as the Justices may direct'. From this time onwards soup, meat and vegetables appear on the daily menu.

The cook was drawn from the ranks of the convicted felons. At meal times the food was served, under the supervision of the storekeeper, into individual wooden dishes which were carried to the various wards. These were distributed according to a ritual similar to that performed on board ship with a view to the elimination of favouritism. Two prisoners, chosen daily according to a rota, would stand back to back. One would hold up each dish in turn calling 'This?' whilst his companion who could to see what was being offered would call out the prisoners' names in random order, the meals being served accordingly.

For the first time some regard was paid to the physical well-being of the prisoners. A good standard of cleanliness was demanded, floors were required to be swept daily and scrubbed weekly. Walls were to be limewashed annually or more frequently if there was an outbreak of disease. Each prisoner was to wash his hands and face daily and to bath as required. The Surgeon was expected to examine all prisoners upon reception. No longer could the Keeper raise his poultry on the premises as was the case at Castle Street, no animals or birds with the exception of the Keeper's watchdog, being permitted.

To assure the spiritual welfare of the prisoners, the Chaplain was required to read prayers every Wednesday and Friday and to preach a sermon every Sunday and on Good Friday and Christmas Day. A measure of the importance of the Chaplain is his salary which until 1842 was equal to that of the Keeper. In addition to his pastoral duties, the Chaplain was also responsible for imparting basic educational instruction to those of the younger prisoners who would in his view benefit thereby.

The Surgeon on the other hand was regarded as of lowly rank. As late as 1833 his salary was only £70 as compared with the Chaplain's £200. A part-time official, he was required to examine each prisoner upon reception and to visit the Gaol regularly to minister to the bodily needs of the inmates. Unfortunately, this important member of the staff does not appear always to have been particularly dedicated to his task as witnessed by the frequency of the complaints recorded by the Visiting Justices concerning his lack of attention to his duties. His first priority would, understandably, have been to his private medical practice, further, his zeal would not have been fired by limited facilities available to him at the Gaol where the admission of patients to the Infirmary was discouraged on the grounds of the expense to the County.

From the Surgeon's reports it is clear that a great many of the prisoners received were undernourished and in poor health prior to committal and deaths from consumption were all too frequent. Disease could spread rapidly and epidemic gastric disorder was often experienced. Scabies, too, was prevalent. Fortunately epidemic diseases of a more serious nature were rare. A measure of the comparative cleanliness of the Gaol is the infrequency of gaol fever (typhus). On the occasions when that terrible disease did appear it was invariably the case that the infected prisoner had contracted the fever prior to his being sent to prison. There was a serious outbreak of smallpox in 1868 when a prisoner suffering from the disease was admitted from Wokingham workhouse. He died and three other prisoners became seriously ill before the outbreak was contained. Following a further outbreak in 1871 inmates and staff were vaccinated and the Warders allowed 'a moderate use of tobacco and beer' during their working hours.

Venereal disease was not uncommon among the prisoners. The frequency with which prostitutes, with whom the larger towns of the County abounded, were committed to prison caused the Visiting Justices to make the following protest in their report to the Midsummer Sessions of 1827:

> The Visiting Justices call attention to the increase in duty to the Surgeon as well as the Matron of the frequent commitment of prostitutes in a diseased state by the Chief Magistrate of the Borough of New Windsor. No less than six came in one day last week making a total of seven at that time, three of whom have been in Gaol but a short time before on a similar commitment and on leaving the Gaol told the Matron, but too truly, that they shall return to her shortly. In fact it is the duty of the Visiting Justices to represent that they are of the opinion that the unfortunate girls are sent for the purpose of curing Venerial [*sic*] Disease.

Peel's Prisons Act of 1835 required 'that female prisoners shall be constantly attended by female officers'. The need for a woman to have the responsibility for the supervision of female prisoners was however recognized long before that time. From his appointment as Keeper in 1815, George Eastaff pleaded with Quarter Sessions for the appointment of a woman to his staff. One suspects that his anxiety was due in some measure to an embarrassing situation which had arisen during the term of office of his predecessor, Mr Knight, whose son, George, was rumoured to have improperly conducted himself with women in custody. A committee of Justices appointed to look into the matter seems to have found some substance in the allegations. Naming two young women, one of whom they considered to have been of remarkably bad character, they banished George from the precincts of the Gaol and reinforced their Order by requiring his father to enter into a bond of £50 which would be forfeit if he allowed him ever again to enter within the gates.

It was not until January, 1819, however that the appointment of a Matron was sanctioned. Over the course of the past four years, the Keeper's servant, Mary Hill, had under the direction of Mrs Eastaff acted as Matron in an unofficial, unpaid capacity. So well did she carry out these duties that not only was she appointed to the staff at a wage of £10 per annum but was further rewarded with the handsome sum of £20 on account of her past services. From that time onwards, it was forbidden for any male person, the Keeper and Turnkeys included, to enter the women's side of the prison unless accompanied by the Matron.

Acting on the belief that reform could be achieved through industry (i.e. that hard work is good for one) the authorities set the prisoners to strenuous but profitable employment. During the early years of the nineteenth century, those sentenced to imprisonment with hard labour were set to saw stone and wood. Later, the able-bodied prisoners were obliged to participate in the exhausting, monotonous routine of the treadmill. Those sentenced to simple imprisonment were given lighter tasks – hurdle making, rug weaving and carving wooden bungs for casks. A few were employed in the garden while others with experience of building crafts were employed in maintenance work. It is recorded that in 1834, a prisoner who was by trade a painter saved the County some £40 by undertaking to decorate and whitewash the premises and was rewarded by an allowance of a daily pint of beer whilst engaged in that task.

To facilitate the control of the inmates and to prevent moral contamination, a régime of strict silence was enforced, at least so far as the male prisoners were concerned. The majority of punishments awarded were for breaches of this rule but whatever the prison staff might do to prohibit communication between prisoners, the overcrowded conditions and shortage of staff in the 1830s made this a vain task. The prisoners of the day had in fact developed a quite efficient sign language. A survival is the word 'snout' which is still the prison slang term for tobacco, a request for which was formerly indicated by touching the nose. The prisoners could generally talk quite freely when in their sleeping quarters. To augment an overburdened staff and to assist in the process of maintaining discipline, certain trusted prisoners were designated Wardsmen and required to act as unpaid Turnkeys. They do not however appear to have been particularly effective in the discharge of their duties as all too frequently they went in fear of their fellows who resented and resisted any exercise of their limited authority.

Although it was required by Statute that the less sophisticated prisoner should be segregated from the hardened offender, the method of classification employed was defective in that it took into account only the nature of the offence in respect of which the prisoner was committed. No distinction was made between the professional thief with a long history of previous convictions and the starving youth tempted into the commission of his first offence. Moreover, the burglar might occasionally be sent to prison for trying his hand at begging, a professional sheep-stealer for doing a little business as a thimblerig man or a London pickpocket for showing fight at a country fair.

Whilst there was a degree of fellow feeling among the prisoners who found themselves thrown together in unhappy circumstances, their charity did not always extend to the newly admitted members of their miniature society. The more timid and inadequate person, particularly if it were his first time in prison, could be treated very roughly. Although the collection of 'garnish', presents of money or valuables to those with whom the new arrival was to share a ward, was officially forbidden, he was sure to be stripped of the few personal possessions which had not already been taken from him, and if he did not conform to the standards of the prison sub-culture, use the prison slang or participate in general profanity, he was sure to be victimized. As likely as not he would find himself dragged before the 'Felons' Court'. One of the more extravert members of the group would don a wig improvised from towelling and sit as

Judge, others would parody the rôle of prosecuting and defend-
ing counsel while the remainder would represent the jury. The
accused might be 'charged' with failing to hand over his money
or be indicted with, say, having red hair and having been found
guilty, as would invariably be the case, would be made the subject of humiliating horseplay. These proceedings would as a
rule take place at night in the sleeping rooms as during the hours
of darkness it was rare for more than one Turnkey to be keeping
watch over the whole of the prison and a little noise would more
often than not go unheeded.

For those who wished to learn the tricks of the criminal profession there were opportunities in plenty. Here, too, the more
sophisticated offenders were able to recruit their disciples.

For the younger prisoners the danger was very great. The
Chaplain, the Rev. Field in a report to Quarter Sessions related
the case of a boy aged 12 years who had been committed to the
prison in 1839 following conviction of passing counterfeit coin:

> Born and brought up in one of the lowest districts of
> London he had been a companion of thieves from infancy.
> He had previously been in Abingdon prison for having on
> the racecourse cut out a woman's pocket and pilfered the
> contents, a feat which he boasted of having frequently
> performed. Whilst in prison he had the opportunity of
> teaching his malpractices to not less than 77 companions.

The Rev. Field was following in the footsteps of his worthy
predecessor, the Rev. Robert Appleton, later to become Head-
master of Reading School, who some five years earlier had in a
lengthy report to Quarter Sessions set forth his views concerning
the treatment of offenders. The first object of punishment, he
said, was not to inflict upon the offender pain proportionate to
his crime but to deter others from committing a like offence. He
advocated a course leading to 'correction and improvement' in
a setting where 'evil tempers and habits will not be drawn forth
and where (the prisoner's) better feelings may be drawn out'.
In his view the offender should be sent to prison *as* a punishment

and not *for* punishment. He was critical in the extreme of the existing regime which threw the comparatively innocent into the company of hardened offenders: 'Thieves and other offenders whose crimes are committed upon property receive the most useful instruction. It is here that the old and wily offender picks up his dupes and obtains proselytes and companions.' He comments, too, upon the use made of the prison's facilities by the rootless and homeless: 'It has been ascertained that vagrants come to gaol for the benefit of the pass; others have subjected themselves to imprisonment for the cure of disease and have timed the period so well that during the period of incarceration they are exonerated from labour'.

Appleton's solution to this state of affairs was the complete isolation of each inmate from the others under conditions of solitary confinement combined with labour and instruction, a regime already in effect in several American prisons. An experiment of that nature was, in fact, being conducted at that time at Abingdon Bridewell 'with very beneficial effects.'

In an age in which any unnecessary expenditure of public funds was viewed with great distaste, he created a sensation by arguing that the question of profit and loss should not be taken into account in this field.

Although the sale of spiritous liquor within the gaol was forbidden as early as 1792, it would appear that the Keeper continued to sell beer well into the nineteenth century. Even after the sale of strong drink in any form was forbidden there is evidence of a fairly brisk clandestine traffic in alcohol for consumption by the prisoners. Games of chance were forbidden but dice were frequently discovered as were packs of cards, some cleverly made from the covers of religious tracts left by the Chaplain for the edification of the prisoners, the markings painted in inks concocted from brick dust and soot. Dominoes, too, were improvised from odd scraps of wood.

Whilst conditions in the gaol during the early years of the nineteenth century were uncomfortable and unhealthy, they were not unduly terrible by the standards of the times and were

St Laurence's Church with Blagrave's Piazza, *c.* **1800:** 'The Hole' is behind the studded door at the end of the arcade. Beside the cell is the enclosure in which the town stocks and ducking stool were stored. To the right of the picture is the Compter House, the residence of the Head Constable and for many years the Magistrates' Court.

Interior of the Borough Bridewell, 1816:
The prisoners slept in cells created by the
partitioning of the side aisle and exercised
and worked in the roofless nave. A dividing
wall separated the male prisoners from the
female. The small building in the centre of
the yard is an earth closet.

Greyfriars Church Reading before restoration 82

The Borough Bridewell: A rare photograph depicting Greyfriars prior to restoration in 1863. Entry to the Bridewell was by the gateway adjacent to the Keeper's house.

The New County Gaol, 1844: A familiar
sight to railway passengers passing through
Reading, the building stood virtually
unchanged until the demolition in August
1971 of the corner turrets and of the
buildings flanking the gate lodge.

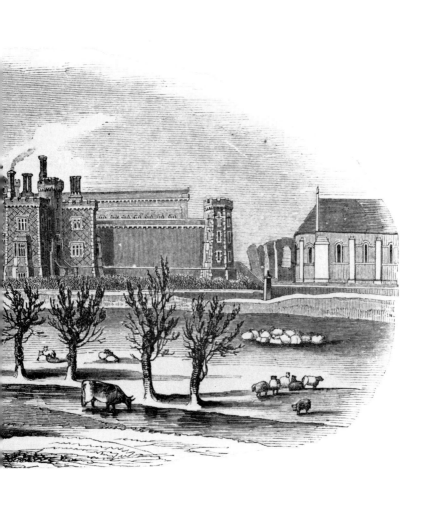

'A' Wing, interior, 1844: From the glazed inspection box
above the entrance, the Warder in charge could command
a view of all that went on in the building. The prisoner on
the right is wearing the face mask and badge.

'C' Wing, interior, 1972: Fluorescent tubes have replaced
the fishtail gas burners and the floors are now plastic tiled.
Otherwise the general appearance has changed little in
130 years.

'E' Wing, the former Women's Prison, 1970: An unusual view from the central tower. The female prisoners who were completely segregated from the males were under the care of the Matron whose rooms were situated in the corner turret.

H.M. Prison, Reading, 1950: The prison before modernization. A view from the south-east.

by all accounts superior to those enjoyed by the private soldier in the British Army.

Upon the appointment in 1834 of Lieut Hackett as Keeper in the place of Thomas Eastaff who resigned following serious criticism by the Justices of his administrative abilities, a thorough reorganization took place. In a report relating to the finances of the gaol, a Visiting Justice writes 'waste, extravagance and unnecessary charges were swept away; and economy and good management supplied in their place'. One of the convicts about that time expressed his feelings in the words 'Good God, they'll be treating us like sojers yet!' Word of the changes in the prison regime spread quickly throughout the county with the result that the number of convicts fell from 121 in October, 1834, to only 65 in October of the following year. In their report to the Michaelmas Sessions of 1835 the Visiting Justices comment:

> This reduction is too large to have been accidental and much of it is ascribed to the improvement that has been introduced into the discipline and the change that has been made in the diet of the Gaol. Under the firm, vigilant and judicious control of Mr Hackett, the Gaol has regained its proper influence as a place of punishment; and it has been a common observation among the prisoners upon their discharge 'that it won't do now to come here anymore'.

The accounts of the period indicate a fall in the cost of maintaining each prisoner from 1s. 6d. per day in 1831 to only 11¾d. in 1835, a reduction of over 30 per cent.

The new gaol was so designed to operate the 'Separate System' whereby each inmate was effectively segregated from his fellows and lived and worked for the greater part of his sentence in his own cell. Not only was all communication between prisoners forbidden but the authorities went to considerable lengths to preserve anonymity among them. From the time of his admission the prisoner was known only by his number which was inscribed on a badge worn on his uniform jacket.

Part of his dress was a cloth cap with a long peak which could be pulled down to cover the face. On those occasions when circumstances dictated that the prisoners should come together it was the rule that the peak should be lowered. Any failure to do this resulted in severe punishment. Solitary confinement was, in all seriousness, imposed as a reformatory device whereby the prisoner should enjoy the benefits of uninterrupted self-communion which it was hoped would lead to repentance and moral regeneration. Whilst it was soon apparent that such a system, far from inculcating spiritual and moral reformation, led to a deterioration in health, a lowering of mental and physical capacity and the most agonizing suffering, it was found to be, of all punishments, the one most dreaded by criminals. Further, of all prison systems, it afforded the least chance of escape and gave the least trouble to the prison staff. It called for the minimum of staff to operate and once the capital cost of the building had been met, was the most economical.

The cells were identical in size and shape. The furnishing and fittings were absolutely standardized and the prisoner was required to lay out his few belongings daily in the prescribed manner. No personal embellishments of any kind were permitted. The prisoner's solitude was broken only by the periodical visits of the Governor, the Chaplain and of the Surgeon.

Life within the gaol was governed by an inflexible timetable which took into account neither the day of the week nor the season of the year except that on Sundays and Holy Days the prisoner went twice to chapel and was expected to spend the remainder of the day in meditation or study instead of at normal labour.

5.30 a.m.	Officers rise.
6.00	Prisoners rise, stow bedding, wash. Unlocked to clean corridors and cells.
8.00	Breakfast.
9.00	Staff muster in Inspection Hall.

9.10	Bell for Chapel. Female prisoners enter by front door and D Wing stairs; males enter from upper gallery.
10.00	Return to cells for labour. Detachments to pumps and to airing yards to air bedding. Schoolmaster's class in Chapel. Surgeon's rounds.
12.00 noon	Prisoners dine. Governor accompanied by Principal Warder visits each cell.
12.30 p.m.	Resume labour. Groups of prisoners to exercise yard for one hour.
6.00	Supper.
7.30	Tools and work materials collected.
7.45	Prisoners prepare for bed. Clothes folded and placed outside cell.
8.00	Bed.

Great store was set upon religious observance and study and during the early years of the operation of the 'Separate System' the prisoners were obliged to spend a great deal of their time committing to memory long passages from the Old and New Testaments.

Writing in 1881, Sir Edmund Du Cane, Chairman of the Prison Commissioners, viewed with scorn the regime in force at Reading Gaol in those early days:

The inmates learned lessons all day except when attending Chapel, exercising, cleaning cells etc. As a privilege they might when tired of reading pick a little oakum but this was quite optional and heavy labour absolutely forbidden in order that the whole establishment might be devoted to literature – the establishment was a criminal university and acquired the name of Read-Read-Reading Gaol.

He goes on to relate how one prisoner having learned by heart the New Testament as far as Ephesians returned on a further sentence to learn the remainder. This was however an exaggerated account ignoring the rationale of the regime which was reformative. The Chaplain of the day, the Rev. John Field, was a firm believer in the value of the Scriptures and was horrified by the 'heathen ignorance' of the majority of the prisoners. Convinced that reformation and religious enlightenment went hand in hand he converted the Justices to the belief that any activity which afforded the prisoners relief from solitude could only impede his task of enforcing repentance and imparting new faith. He also persuaded them that labour of any kind was a mistake as a man with nothing to do would be only too glad to accept an invitation to read the Bible or be taught to read it – if only to save himself from going mad. It was not long before the prisoner population tumbled to the fact that a sure way to win the approval of the Chaplain was to develop an ability to learn and to recite lengthy passages from the Bible and to express the deepest contrition for one's past depravity.

In April, 1862, an Indian Student, Rakhal Das Haldar, whose travels brought him temporarily to Reading, visited the gaol and recorded these impressions in his diary:

> Returned to the house of Mr Howse for a while and then the two brothers H. and I went to the Jail. It is an improved model Jail: looks from the outside more like a splendid college than anything else. Tidiness marks most things English, and even when we had entered the building we could hardly believe ourselves within prison walls; such is our general idea of a prison. Having waited a minute or two in a neat little room, a warder bade us follow him; and we passed on to the centre of the building which is erected in the form of a cross. From the centre you see vistas in four directions, lighted by the entrance door or large windows at the furthest ends. The prisoners

were engaged in work, each having a mask on his face.
They are not allowed to exchange a word or look with
each other, and the building is accordingly constructed. In
each room, works a solitary prisoner. There is room for
twenty men performing exercises without seeing each other.
The cells contain such articles of furniture as are absolutely
necessary; there is good ventilation; whenever the prisoner
wants anything, he rings the bell, and it is so admirably
arranged, that the moment the bell rings, a plate of brass
projects from the wall outside; and as the number of the
prisoner is marked on the plate, the warder has no
difficulty to know by whom he is called. There are excellent
baths and the prisoner is allowed to bathe once every
month. The building is supplied with water, heat etc. by
a steam engine; the temperature allowed to the prisoners is
about 50 °Fahr. We then passed down to the kitchen which
was as clean as could be wished (in fact English kitchens
are very different things from our dark, dingy and smoky
rooms). As to diet, three meals are allowed during the day.
Males have 8 oz. (marked) bread, and females 6 oz. each
time. The bread is brown of course, but we thought
sufficiently good. Breakfast (8 a.m.) consists of bread and
gruel. Dinner (1 p.m.) consists of bread and meat; and tea
(5 p.m.) consists of bread and tea. Rice and potatoes
are allowed as vegetables. I examined the rice and found
it to be good. Whenever the surgeon recommends,
extra diet is given. Saw some excellent mats of coconut
fibre sold at market price. Prisoners are employed on
more or less hard work according to their physical
capacity. There is a chapel above; the pews so arranged
that the prisoners cannot communicate with one another
while everyone is within sight of the chaplain. The
governors, the chaplains, the surgeon and the teachers visit
the prisoners as often as every day. Refractory prisoners are
condemned to the gloomy cells and to reduced diet. The
warder said that not unfrequently do some of them prove

refractory. My visit to the Jail impressed me with the idea of the great improvements made in criminal jurisprudence within the last thirty years.

A further Prisons Act was passed in 1865 following a review of the working of the prison system by a Select Committee of the House of Lords. Reflecting the concern currently being voiced at the apparent increase in violent crime, the new legislation brought about a tightening of prison 'discipline'. Imprisonment with hard labour having by this time become the standard punishment prescribed by law for all felonies other than those punishable by death, and for many misdemeanours as well, the Berkshire Justices were obliged to scrap their programme of moral rehabilitation through Biblical study and to substitute arduous physical labour. Unwilling to reintroduce the treadwheel, they looked to stonebreaking as 'a means of punishment with profitable results'. For the first three months of his sentence the prisoner who had been sentenced to a term of Hard Labour spent his days in the stoneyard breaking flint and granite for sale to the highway authorities for use as road-metal, the principal customer being Reading Corporation. Having undergone his period of hard physical labour, the prisoner would spend the next six months in cellular confinement engaged in 'useful labour'. The unskilled would pick oakum or grind corn by means of the hand-operated mills whilst those blessed with manual dexterity and some experience might be put to tailoring, shoemaking or matmaking. Female prisoners would work in the laundry or at knitting or mending prison clothing.

Influenced by agitation concerning the allegedly excessive amounts of food given to prisoners as compared with workhouse inmates and soldiers, the Home Office laid down a revised scale of prison dietary from which the county could not depart even had the Visiting Justices so desired. This move was in fact welcomed by the Justices who saw the deterrent aspect of imprisonment reinforced together with a saving to the ratepayers. It being felt that meat was at that time a luxury rarely attainable by the poor but honest labourer, both meat and soup were dropped from the menu as were leeks, onions and rice. For the next thirty years the scale of rations would be as follows:

CLASS 1 (Prisoners serving 7 days or under)

Breakfast	1 pint gruel, 4 oz. bread
Dinner	6 oz. bread
Supper	6 oz. bread

CLASS 2 (Sentences of 8 to 21 days)

| Breakfast and supper | 1 pt gruel, 6 oz. bread |
| Dinner | 8 oz. potatoes, 4 oz. bread |

CLASS 3 (Sentences of 22 to 42 days)

| Breakfast and supper | 1 pt gruel, 6 oz. bread |
| Dinner | 8 oz. potatoes, 8 oz. bread |

CLASS 4 (Sentences exceeding 42 days)

| Breakfast and supper | 1 pt gruel, 6 oz. bread |

Dinner – Sunday
   Tuesday
   Thursday   8 oz. bread, 1 lb. potatoes,
   Saturday   2 oz. cheese

   Monday
   Wednesday   8 oz. bread, 1 lb. potatoes,
   Friday   3 oz. bacon

All prisoners with the exception of those serving less than one week were fed upon reception according to Class 2 progressing after three weeks to Class 3. Having completed six weeks of his sentence, the prisoner would receive the rations accorded to Class 4. The above quantities were applicable to adult males only, women and boys under the age of 14 years being allowed 4 oz. bread at each meal.

The reduction in the dietary scale, always an explosive area in prison life, was effected without too much trouble. A dissenting voice was that of J. G. Perry, one of the Inspectors of Prisons, who felt that the new scale of food was far from nutritious. He was particularly critical of the absence of meat. His comments were largely disregarded although it was following his protest that the prisoners in Class 1 were allowed the luxury of a pint of warm gruel for breakfast.

The year 1877 saw the nationalization of the prisons and the following year Reading Gaol was formally handed over to the Prison Commissioners.

Responsibility for the management and maintenance of the prisons having passed to the Crown, all property supplied for use within the establishment was branded with the mark of the broad arrow indicating its official origin. All items of prison clothing were clearly marked in this way, not so much as an indication of ownership but as an aid to identification should the wearer happen to stray.

The new regime was harsh in that all prisoners were reduced to the same level with no concession as to personal circumstances. Individuality was just not recognized. There were however a few beneficial changes, numbered among which was a relaxation of the 'Separate System' to which the County Justices had adhered for so long. Although the prisoners were still not permitted to associate out of working hours or even to converse, they were brought together for employment. The wearing of the mask was also abolished it being recognized at long last that the prison community is so close that the mere hiding of a prisoner's face did nothing to hide his identity.

It was the intention of the Commissioners that the rigour of the discipline to which the prisoner was subject should be in some degree in his own hands. Upon reception into prison he would be regarded as a member of the First Stage and would receive few concessions as to his comfort. By means of the award of marks appropriate to his behaviour and industry he would gain promotion through three further stages.

The first twenty eight days of a prisoner's sentence were spent in the First Stage during which time he was obliged to spend ten hours daily engaged in First Class Hard Labour. At Reading Prison where there was no treadmill, hard labour involved such tasks as stonebreaking with a heavy hammer, raising water by means of the crank-operated pump, the grinding of corn by patent hand mill, mat making, weaving on the heavy loom and rope-beating. These jobs were performed in strict silence if segregation were impracticable.

Points for industry and good behaviour were awarded daily to a maximum of 8. To earn elevation to the Second Stage, the prisoner was obliged to earn a total of 224 points (i.e. 28 × 8). Having attained the Second Stage, he would be assigned lighter duties designated Second Class Hard Labour. In this category was included the boring and painful task of picking oakum – the unravelling of old rope to produce a fibre employed in the process of caulking the seams of wooden ships. The prisoner was denied the use of a 'fid', a metal hook to assist in the shredding of tarred or knotted pieces of rope and had to rely upon the strength and hardness of his fingers. Other tasks were tailoring, shoemaking, painting, whitewashing and the less attractive domestic duties of the prison. A prisoner in the Second Stage was allowed the luxury of a mattress twice weekly and would be released from his cell to exercise on Sunday. He could also earn a gratuity not exceeding 1s. payable upon discharge.

Having earned a total of 448 points the prisoner would be admitted to the Third Stage which would entitle him to the use of a mattress on six nights of the week and to receive library books. He could earn a gratuity not exceeding 1s. 6d.

A prisoner serving a sentence of over three months could, having earned at least 672 marks, spend the remainder of his sentence in the Fourth Stage. He would by this time be eligible for employment demanding a degree of trust and could qualify for a gratuity not exceeding 10s. His additional privileges would include, in addition to the use of a mattress every night, permission to write and to receive one letter every three months and to receive a visit of up to 20 minutes in duration at similar intervals.

Misbehaviour or even a lack of effort on the part of a prisoner could result in an Order by the Visiting Justices for the forfeiture of gratuity, forfeiture of marks or of reduction to a lower Stage.

These were not, of course, the only punishments that could be meted out for breaches of prison discipline. For the most minor transgression a prisoner would be placed on report and brought before the Governor who could award punishment by way of confinement in a bare cell with plank bed and wooden pillow or in a totally dark cell with a diet of bread and water for up to three days at a time. The Visiting Justices were empowered to order such confinement for a period as long as fourteen days.

For more serious offences, the Visiting Magistrates could order corporal punishment by way of the birch or the cat o' nine tails. The 'cat' was a fearsome instrument. Attached to a wooden handle were nine strings of whipcord each 23 in. long with a single knot in the end. The prisoner to be punished would be tied to a wooden triangle and the flogging administered in the presence of the Governor and the Surgeon by the Warder on duty. In response to a questionnaire issued by the Home Secretary in 1860, William Merry, the Chairman of the Visiting Justices replied that 'punishment by whipping is never resorted to until after all other means of remonstrance, warning and minor punishment have been tried in vain. Then we consider that if a man will not see the reason he has been gifted with by Providence he reduces himself to the level of an animal and must be dealt with by animal law.'

Whilst flogging does not appear to have been ordered with undue frequency, the penalty when imposed was severe as one may judge from the following entries from the Justices' Order Book:

7 June 1862   James Crew, a lad of 16 in prison for third Felony, too old for a reformatory school, having been punished for repeated offences

is brought before the Visiting Justices for refractory conduct. 12 lashes. Birch.

10 June 1865   Johnson, a prisoner many times in prison, sentenced to be flogged for violent misconduct. 24 lashes.

23 Dec. 1865   Jas Eiles ordered to be whipped 1 doz for tearing up his clothing, breaking window and damaging bason.

6 June 1866   Johnson was ordered to receive two dozen lashes for striking Warder Brewer in the execution of his duty.

25 Jan. 1868   Wm Kent age 17 who has been in this Gaol before and now transferred from Abingdon charged with loosening the bricks of his cell, probably with a view to escape. A few days since he eluded the vigilance of the Warders and was not found till after a long search. To be flogged, 12 lashes.

That recalcitrance might originate from mental disorder was not always appreciated and a persistent offender against prison discipline ran the risk of heavy handed treatment:

1 Jan. 1881   589 George Cox reported for improper conduct in the Chapel on Xmas Day in climbing over the rails of the top corridor and letting himself down to the pavement below. This prisoner was also reported for 'destroying articles of Government property and for grossly indecent and disgusting conduct in the presence of the Governor.' Ordered to receive 18 strokes of the birch.

8 Jan. 1881   For wilful damage to property and for a repetition of the disgusting conduct to the Governor and Warders ordered 2 dozen lashes with the cat.

15 Jan. 1881   Cox again before the Visiting Justices for destroying his clothing and generally smashing up the furniture and fittings of his cell.

On the latter occasion the Surgeon expressed the opinion that this man's mental condition was such that he did not advise detention in a dark cell. By this time the Justices also had come to the conclusion that further corporal punishment was inadvisable and directed the Governor to keep Cox in his own cell taking all the precautions possible against further offences.

In 1884 it was the turn of John Whittaker:

21 June 1884   A2.24 John Whittaker having attempted to commit suicide and having refused to take his food, the Visiting Committee directed that he should be reduced to the First Stage with hard labour [i.e. a reduction in priviledges of all kinds]. Warned that he would be placed in a dark cell if he persisted.

5 July 1884   Brought before the Visiting Committee for refusing to take his food and to work *and on the recommendation of the Surgeon* [my italics] ordered to receive 25 lashes.

12 July 1884   Again before the Visiting Committee charged with refusing to take his food. Ordered that he should receive 36 lashes, the punishment to be at the discretion of the Governor and conditional upon his persistence in the same conduct. [There is no record of this order having been put into effect.]

1 Nov. 1884   Charged with damaging various articles in his cell and using obscene language. To be deprived of two good conduct badges.

8 Nov. 1884   Again reported for refusing to leave his cell and to go to work on Thursday and Friday. To be confined in a dark cell for 48 hours.

Until the total abolition of corporal punishment in prisons by virtue of the Criminal Justice Act of 1967, the Visiting Justices had the power to order the flogging of offenders against discipline and good order within the establishment. During the nineteenth century their powers were virtually unlimited although the Surgeon who was obliged to witness the punishment could order a halt if in his opinion the prisoner was unable to withstand further pain. With the passing of the Prison Act, 1898, the range of offences which attracted corporal punishment was limited to those involving mutiny or gross personal violence to a member of the prison staff and all such adjudications had to be confirmed by the Secretary of State before being put into effect.

A graphic account of life in Reading Gaol during the latter years of the nineteenth century is presented by Oscar Wilde in two letters to the *Daily Chronicle*. The first of these appeared on the 28 May 1897, less than a fortnight after his release, and refers to the case of Warder Martin before going on to deal with the rigidity and inhumanity of the prison regime of the day. His second letter was published on 24 March 1898, at the time of the consideration by Parliament of the Prison Reform Bill. 'The necessary Reforms', says Wilde, 'are very simple and concern the needs of the body and the needs of the mind of each unfortunate prisoner.' 'But,' he cautions, 'to make these effectual, much has to be done. And the first, and perhaps most difficult task, is to humanize the Governors of prisons, to civilize the warders and to Christianize the chaplains.'

Having enjoyed comfortable material circumstances throughout his life and, further, having been committed to prison for behaviour which he did not regard as criminal, Wilde found the experience traumatic in the extreme. His account of his own prison life in his essay *De Profundis* and in these letters to the Press, whilst subjective, is not too greatly distorted.

The food supplied to prisoners, he complains, is quite insufficient and most of it revolting in character – weak gruel, suet and water. Perhaps the aspect of prison life which revolted him the most was the lack of adequate sanitary facilities:

Nothing can be worse than the sanitary arrangements of
English prisons. In the old days each cell was provided
with a form of latrine. These latrines have now been
suppressed. A small tin vessel is supplied to each prisoner
instead. Three times a day a prisoner is allowed to empty
his slops. But he is not allowed to have access to the prison
lavatories, except during one hour when he is at exercise.
And after five o'clock in the evening he is not allowed to
leave his cell under any pretence, or for any reason. . . .
And the foul air of the prison cells, increased by a system
of ventilation that is utterly ineffective is so unwholesome
that it is no uncommon thing for warders, when they come
on in the morning out of the fresh air and open and inspect
each cell, to be violently sick.

Wilde goes on to comment that as one is only allowed out of
one's cell for one hour out of the twenty-four, for the remaining
twenty-three one breathes the foulest of air. To add to the claus-
trophobic atmosphere, the cell windows were small, heavily
barred and set high in the wall. These could not be opened
and the only communication with the fresh air was a small,
sliding ventilator pane.

A gregarious, extraverted person, Wilde found the enforced
segregation from his fellows hard to bear and recommended that
each prisoner should be allowed a supply of good books.

At present, during the first three months of imprisonment,
one is allowed no books at all, except a Bible, Prayer Book
and hymn book. After that one is allowed one book a week.
That is not merely inadequate but the books that compose
an ordinary prison library are perfectly useless. They consist
chiefly of badly written, third rate religious books, so
called, written apparently for children, and utterly
unsuitable for children or for anyone else. At present, the
selection of books is made by the prison chaplain.

At this time a prisoner was allowed to write and to receive only
four letters a year. It was a strict rule that incoming correspon-

dence should refer only to family and personal matters, any reference to current events would be deleted by being cut out with a pair of scissors. Outgoing correspondence was also rigidly censored and any complaint concerning the prison or any other matter which the Governor considered improper would be similarly suppressed. Visits, likewise, were limited to four a year. At Reading Gaol these took place in the Visiting Room in D Wing where both prisoner and visitor sat behind a wire mesh grille some three or four feet apart with a Warder between to monitor the conversation. A prisoner to be interviewed by his solicitor would, however, enjoy better facilities in an adjoining room where, as in present-day practice, the visit took place within the sight but out of the hearing of a Warder who kept observation through a glass door.

Wilde records that children, whether those remanded in custody awaiting trial or those sentenced to a term of imprisonment, were treated little differently from the adult prisoners. They, too, were subject to strict segregation and were allowed but one hour's exercise a day. They, too, received the same diet as adults. Perhaps the only concession to their years was the attempt to isolate them from the sight of the adults by arranging for them to exercise in the stoneyard and by placing them behind a curtain whilst in chapel.

The cruelty encountered in prison, says Wilde, does not result from any conscious intent but arises from stereo-typed systems, hard-and-fast rules and from stupidity.

> The people who uphold the system have excellent intentions. Those who carry it out are humane in intention also. Responsibility is shifted on to the disciplinary regulations. It is supposed that because a thing is a rule it is right.

It is appropriate at this point to say a little concerning life today at H.M. Prison, Reading. Whilst the interior arrangement of the building has changed little since it was built, the process of modernization and refurbishment has brought with it an air of brightness and cleanliness which is apparent as soon as one enters. The enlarged cell windows admit a greater degree of light and fresh air than was possible in the past, while the brighter decoration takes away the harshness of the brickwork. The globeless gas jet has given way to two-strength fluorescent lighting which can be operated by the prisoner from within his cell as well as by the Officer on the landing outside. The cell furniture whilst simple is of a colourful, modern design and includes a pin board upon which the inmate may mount photographs and pictures of his choice – provided always that they are not too lurid. Instead of the plank bed and coir mattress, he now sleeps on foam rubber.

Although it is a case of one prisoner to a cell, he is locked in only at night and for a very brief period during the day. The restriction of communication between prisoners has long since been abolished and the emphasis is now on the development of satisfactory personal relationships within the group as part of the process of social re-education. A reasonable amount of talking is permitted whilst at work and there is freedom to associate during meal-times and in the evenings.

The policy that work for prisoners should be punitive, and therefore as purposeless and degrading as possible has long since been abandoned. The range of employment offered is at the present time restricted on account of lack of workshop facilities, a shortcoming which will be remedied within the near future upon the completion of a modern complex which would excite the envy of any light industrialist. At the time of writing the prisoners are engaged in the dismembering of scrap electrical apparatus in order to recover copper and the more precious metals, light assembly work and the production of mailbags. A few of the more intelligent men are employed in the analysis of weather charts for the Meteorological Office and an experiment is being undertaken in the recording of advanced textbooks for the use of blind students. Other men are employed on domestic duty as cleaners and assistants in the kitchen and Officers' Mess.

Food in prison remains a subject of the greatest importance. Whilst the Catering Officer is obliged to work within the framework of a strict budget, the food which he prepares is both nutritious and imaginative. Monotony of diet is avoided and care is taken to ensure that the food is properly served. The prisoner receives three cooked meals daily with the addition of a supper snack, all of which compare favourably with those served in hospitals and similar institutions. Bread is still baked on the premises although needless to say the flour is no longer ground by the prisoners.

Prison clothing is grey and still somewhat shapeless. There are of course problems in providing serviceable clothing to suit all members of a population the turnover of which is rapid and whose members come in all shapes and sizes. Shirts, socks and underwear are of a modern pattern and are laundered frequently. Suitable boots or shoes are provided for work but slippers may be worn during leisure hours.

An extremely well equipped gymnasium, a legacy from the period in 1950 when the establishment was a Borstal Institution, is placed at the disposal of the prisoners. Under the eye of a qualified Physical Education Instructor, offenders who are not fully fit can receive remedial training and gymnastics; others may participate in circuit training, weight lifting, gymnastics and indoor sports.

Education has an important part to play in the training process. For the illiterate and the backward, there are remedial classes at which attendance is compulsory. There are in the evenings a selection of courses in subjects which range from advanced academic standards to matters of general interest – modern languages, accountancy, first aid light handicrafts and art to quote but a few. Religious observance is encouraged although there is no longer any compulsion upon the prisoner to attend Chapel. Members of the various denominations may be visited by the Minister of their own particular sect and services are held on Sunday and on other occasions of religious significance in the small but attractive 'Chapel of the Upper Room' situated at the front of the building. The former nineteenth-century chapel being too large by far for present-day needs, now serves as a visiting area.

There is a particular place for the professional Welfare Officer, a Probation Officer seconded for service in the prison. It is truly said that if prisoners share a single common factor it is their propensity to attract problems to themselves. The Welfare Officer therefore has an obvious role in affording both 'first aid' help with social and family problems as well as attempting social casework in depth. Among his responsibilities is the task of assisting the homeless and isolated prisoner to forge new links with the outside world and of supporting other inmates in maintaining satisfactory communication with home and family throughout the course of the sentence.

'Good Order and Discipline' must of necessity be maintained and there are rules and regulations which must be observed on pain of sanction. Discipline however rests more upon the attitudes towards each other of the staff and of the prisoners in their charge than upon the machinery of enforcement and the uniformed Officer is encouraged to get to know and to understand the men in his charge. To this end he is brought into the area of decision-making in the field of treatment and his views are invariably taken into consideration.

The wheel would have appeared to have turned full circle since the days of the silent and separate systems. Methods of treatment have changed but the basic aim is still the same, to bring the offender to a realization that whilst Society has expressed its displeasure at his conduct, it is not beyond his power to amend his behaviour.

7 THE PRISONERS

Whilst there is a record of the name, age and offence of each prisoner who has passed through the gates of Reading Gaol, the official rolls, unhappily for the historian, tell us little of their personal circumstances. Who then were the prisoners? What events led to their enforced loss of freedom?

Volumes have already been written concerning the causes of crime and the characteristics of the criminal and it is not within the compass of this book to enlarge upon the theories already advanced. Suffice it to say that the prisoner is a person who has come into conflict with the standards and values of the society of his day and as a result has been banished therefrom. His imprisonment may have been ordered to remove a potentially or actually dangerous or disruptive influence from that society; it is however more likely that the punishment was imposed to deter others who might be tempted to behave in a similar manner.

The archetypal image of the prisoner is still strong in the imagination of the man in the street and is perpetuated by the newspaper cartoonist; beetle-browed and bulldog-jawed, he dresses when at liberty in a flat cap, striped jersey and mask and over his shoulder carries a bag marked 'swag'. When the time comes for him to 'pay his debt to society' he exchanges that uniform for a shapeless suit of grey adorned with broad arrows. There are in reality no physical stigmata which distinguish the offender from his apparently law abiding brethren. Crime is however predominantly the activity of the young male. That this hypothesis is sound, is borne out by the statistics relating to the inmates of Reading Gaol over the past century and a half. The majority of the prisoners have been under the age of 25 years whilst men have outnumbered women by about ten to one. It must however be borne in mind that certain types of crime – false pretences by way of example – are classless and can persist into advanced age whilst certain kinds of vagrancy and offences against public order are the province of the older person who has failed completely to establish himself in an acceptable way of life and sees prison as a kind of haven from the troubles of an unsympathetic world. There are yet others who, whilst physically and mentally unfitted to function satisfactorily in society, are nevertheless, deemed medically sane and are treated as 'bad' rather than 'mad'.

Let us however leave the realms of criminology and return to the historical perspective.

By the later years of the eighteenth century, the rule of law was strong. Almost as powerful as that of Parliament was the sway of the Justices of the Peace whose patriarchal oversight encompassed almost every aspect of everyday life in England. In the rural areas, the Justices were invariably men of substance, landowners and squires, proud to undertake public office without payment and who were very much a law unto themselves. Not only were they required by a Statute of 1361 to 'pursue, arrest, take and chastise offenders', they were also responsible for the general administration of their locality, for the construction and maintenance of fortifications, highways, bridges, workhouses and gaols and for raising the necessary money and labour for the purpose. Their powers were extensive and they used them to the full. In dealing with breaches of the law there are instances of ferocious punishments being inflicted by their order. There is however no reason to suppose that the men who enforced the laws were any more brutal than those who made them, or that either group was much out of accord with the moral climate and culture of the age.

In a society ruled by men of property it is understandable that the laws relating to the protection of material goods should be strict. There being no effective police force to protect property and to detect wrongdoers, harsh penalties were imposed upon those who were caught in order to deter others from a similar course of behaviour. The heavier the punishment, the greater the degree of deterrence it was believed. The alarming increase in the ranks of the poor and the marked decline in the respect of the lower classes for their social superiors was a constant threat which caused those invested with civil powers to close their ranks. By 1800, there was upon the Statute Book a total of no less than 220 offences punishable by death. Among the capital offences was the theft of property to the value of one shilling or over. This was not however an age of complete inhumanity and Juries would often refuse to convict an offender accused of a minor crime, conviction in respect of which would lead to the gallows.

The prosecuting authorities, too, were not unaware of the grave consequences of conviction and would sometimes frame charges in such a way as not to attract the capital penalty but would proceed in a manner which would lead to nothing more serious than a prison sentence or perhaps a whipping. The ready method of attaining this end was to value the property to which the charge related at a sum just a little less than that which brought it within the scope of a capital offence:

Midsummer Sessions, 1791 :
Joseph Bedford of Newbury. Guilty of stealing 6 fowls valued 10*d*. Ordered to be publicly whipped at Newbury and imprisoned for three months in a solitary cell at the Reading House of Correction.

During the time of the French wars a convicted offender, if able bodied, could avoid imprisonment by 'volunteering' for service in the Royal Navy.

Michaelmas Sessions, 1796 :
John Smith of Windsor – pleaded not guilty but convicted of stealing a pig 'commonly called a Barrow Pig' of the price of 10*d*. To be confined for two years the last month in a close cell unless he enters His Majesty's Service.

William Lucas found guilty of the theft of 5 chickens value 10*d*. To be imprisoned 2 months with hard labour unless he enters His Majesty's Service.

At the Easter Sessions of 1797, one John Hawkins who had been committed to Reading Gaol on a strong suspicion of stealing a horse was not even called to stand his trial but was ordered by the Court to be sent into the Sea Service.

The general distrust of strangers, particularly those from foreign parts, prevailing at this time is illustrated by a brief entry in the records of the Epiphany Sessions of 1800:

A Lascar and another foreigner who it is presumed is a native of India sent from Reading Gaol to the Hospital or Repository for those people belonging to the East India Company.

It would appear that the two coloured men were found wandering in Wokingham and brought before the Mayor who committed them forthwith to gaol. Their command of the English language was poor but it was possible to ascertain from them that they had come from London having disembarked from a ship, believed to be the East Indiaman *Hibernia*.

By 1808, the Government had been persuaded to substitute the sentence of Transportation for that of hanging as the penalty for some forms of theft and minor dishonesty and to modify the severity of the penal code to some extent.

At the Michaelmas Sessions of 1829, Isaac Neville who had been found guilty of stealing a cloth coat to the value of 20*s*. was sentenced to one month's imprisonment with hard labour and ordered to be twice privately whipped. A few years previously he would have gone to the gallows as would Belcher Lee of Clewer who at the same Sessions was sent to prison with hard labour for 12 months for stealing an ass valued at 18*s*.

Whilst a first offender was in peril of quite severe punishment, a persistent offender could expect little less than the full displeasure of the Court:

Midsummer Sessions, 1830:
Thomas Case, previously convicted of theft at Newbury
Quarter Sessions of October, 1828, and further convicted
in May, 1830, of stealing three neck cloths value 1s. was
convicted of stealing a handkerchief value 6d. together with
3s. in cash. Ordered to be transported for life to such of
His Majesty's Dominions beyond the Seas as His Majesty
by and with the advice of the Privy Council shall order and
direct.

Midsummer Sessions, 1843:
Charles Oakley of Swallowfield in the County of Wilts,*
labourer who on the 26th May of that year stole a
handkerchief of the value of 6d. the property of William
Oakley ordered to be transported for 7 years.

Although disturbance was generally dealt with by requiring
the aggressor to enter into a surety as to his future good behaviour, disorderly conduct could result in a prison sentence as
James Batt and James Carter of Aldermaston discovered when
in 1829 they were convicted of rioting and pulling down a booth.
Sent to prison for three months, it was ordered that they should
spend the first and last weeks of the sentence in solitary confinement.

In England, even during the most troubled times, the political
prisoner is a comparative rarity. He can prove most troublesome
to his custodian, particularly if his supporters are numerous or
if it is widely felt that he has been afforded a raw deal at the
hands of those who have ordered his detention. Three such men
who came to be known as 'The Manchester prisoners' were
instrumental in visiting more anxiety upon the Keeper than he
ever imagined possible.

In the years following the Napoleonic wars, the widespread
economic depression and the high price of food caused much

* At this time the village of Swallowfield and the surrounding area
was regarded as part of Wiltshire.

suffering and distress throughout the country. In the industrial North the people's dissatisfaction found an outlet in rioting and other forms of violence and an attempt to overthrow the established society through bloody revolution was a very real threat. The machinery of government, the function of which was to preserve the *status quo,* although severely overburdened, cast its net as widely as possible in an attempt to silence and put down troublemakers and subversives. It was against this background that on 10 April 1819, George Eastaff, the Keeper of the County Gaol, received three prisoners named Knight, Sellars and Hutton. The trio, residents of Manchester, had been arrested and committed to prison on the instructions of the Home Secretary, Viscount Sidmouth. Accused but not convicted of conspiracy and of using seditious language, they were sent to Reading on a warrant requiring that they should be detained until released by due process of law or for as long as the Minister should please. It was further ordered that they should be lodged in separate cells and kept *incommunicado.* They were not to be permitted pen, ink or paper, to read books or newspapers and no person, not even a Magistrate, was to visit them without the Lord Sidmouth's prior authority.

The weeks slowly passed without any word from the Minister as to what action he proposed to take in respect of the 'State prisoners' and on 30 June, Lord Folkestone, one of the Visiting Justices called at the Gaol demanding to see them. Refused admittance by a Keeper mindful of his instructions, Lord Folkestone was justifiably annoyed and raised the matter in Parliament. His anger was by no means mollified when he was informed that the gaols were the property of the King and that under the Habeas Corpus Suspension Act, which had but recently been brought into effect, the King's Ministers might detain whom they please. Undaunted, Lord Folkestone complained to the Berkshire Quarter Sessions quoting an earlier Act of Parliament empowering a Magistrate to visit and inspect any gaol within the County upon the Commission of the Peace of which he was enrolled. At the Michaelmas Sessions of that year Mr Eastaff was accordingly summoned before the Court and severely reprimanded whilst Lord Folkestone duly exercised his right to visit the prisoners.

Mr Eastaff was in a quandary. Torn between the County Justices who were, after all, his employers and the Home Secretary, the terms of whose warrant he was obliged by law to honour, he acquainted Lord Sidmouth with his problem and requested further instructions. The Home Secretary reiterated his original order – that no one was to have access to the Manchester Prisoners without his express permission, the Order of Quarter Sessions notwithstanding. A week later Lord Folkestone called at the gaol only to be refused access to the prisoners whom he had come to visit. This apparent flouting of their authority was seen by the Justices, who felt that their independence of action was in danger, as a matter of the gravest importance. It was clear to all that a major row was brewing. There was a great deal of activity behind the scenes, the Minister going so far as to create Dr Barry, Rector of Wallingford, a J.P. in order to swing the balance in his favour. The matter having been heatedly discussed in Quarter Sessions, it was determined by 17 votes to 13 that Mr Eastaff should be tried for failing in his duty. He was accordingly suspended from his post without pay, required to vacate his quarters within the prison and bailed to appear before the next Assizes.

The charge against Mr Eastaff was finally heard at the Berkshire Assizes of 3 March 1820 before Mr Justice Park. The case was energetically argued and after a hearing lasting some ten hours the Jurors found in favour of the Keeper whom they felt had acted according to law in following the directions of the Home Secretary. His honour restored, George Eastaff was duly reinstated and served for several years more as Keeper of the County Gaol.

There is unfortunately little information concerning the subsequent fate of the prisoners around whom this controversy raged. It is recorded that Sellers and Knight were released on Christmas Day, 1820, and one assumes that they returned to their homes whilst Knight was sometime removed to Ilchester Gaol.

Charged with High Treason, Roderick Maclean, an artist aged 27 years, was not a political prisoner in the strictest sense. The offence in respect of which he was brought before a special session of the Berkshire Assizes, presided over by no less a personage than Lord Coleridge, Lord Chief Justice of England, was that of attempting to bring about the death of Queen Victoria by firing at her a pistol loaded with gunpowder and a bullet. Maclean's attempt to assassinate the Queen, the sixth and last to which she was subject during her long reign, took place on Thursday, 2 March 1882, at Windsor Railway Station.

Late that afternoon the Queen accompanied by Princess Beatrice and members of the Royal Household arrived in Windsor having travelled from Paddington in the Royal Train. As the party left the station for the Castle in the coaches sent for the purpose a shot was fired from a range of about thirty paces by a man, poorly dressed and of wretched appearance, armed with a revolver. Before a second shot could be fired the would-be assassin was disarmed and arrested. He was indeed saved by the Police from summary vengeance at the hands of the crowd which had witnessed the incident.

Following his arrest, Maclean said that he acted as he did because he was starving. Remanded in custody to Reading Gaol it soon became apparent that he was of unsound mind and subject to the delusion that the public had banded together to do him an injury. Found not guilty on the grounds of insanity the Order of the Court was that he be kept in strict custody until Her Majesty's pleasure be known. He was accordingly returned to the Gaol to await his removal to the Criminal Lunatic Asylum at Broadmoor where, suffering from a condition which would in all probability have today been diagnosed as paranoid schizophrenia, he spent the remainder of his days.

In 1834, the working of the Poor Law was overhauled and the resultant Poor Law Amendment Act introduced a diversity of treatments for the various classes of pauper. The new legislation was intended to deter the able bodied poor who, whilst physically capable of supporting themselves, were content to rely upon public assistance. Outdoor relief in the way of grants of money or foodstuffs was no longer to be afforded persons other than the very young, the sick, and the elderly and those without the means of subsistence were obliged to enter the casual ward of the local workhouse where conditions were made uncongenial in order to discourage applications for admission. Offences against the rules of the workhouse were now regarded as a breach of the criminal law and a new category of offender makes an appearance in the register of prisoners. The most common offence against the discipline of the workhouse was the refusal of the inmate to perform his allotted 'task' which generally entailed breaking stones or picking a quantity of oakum. The usual penalty was a term of 7 or 14 days' imprisonment although disorderly conduct or an assault upon a workhouse official could attract a month's hard labour.

From 1834 until the closure of the prison in 1915 there seems never to have been a day when the gaol did not contain at least one offender against workhouse discipline. There is little doubt that the experienced vagrant found conditions in prison far more satisfactory than those in the workhouse, a fact concerning which the Governor, Capt. Wisden, commented in his report to the Prison Commissioners for the year 1909–10. These men, he said, with few exceptions when once in prison completed their daily task and gave no trouble whatsoever. It was his view that many men went into the casual ward with the deliberate intention of committing some minor offence in order to enjoy the comparative comfort of prison. His suggested solution to this state of affairs was for conditions in the casual wards of the workhouses to be brought into line with those of the prisons.

The coming of the Great Western Railway with its huge gangs of navvies and contractors' labourers, men who worked like slaves under the very worst of conditions and who celebrated their fortnightly pay-day with hard drinking and near riotous behaviour, filled the gaol during the years 1837–40. Very few of these men being natives of Berkshire, the County Justices felt it wrong that the cost of accommodating these men whilst in prison should fall upon the ratepayers. Unfortunately, neither the Railway company nor the contractors would acknowledge responsibility for the behaviour of their employees in their off-duty hours and no financial help was forthcoming from those quarters.

The bargees plying the Kennet and Avon Canal were frequently before the Courts as a result of their leisure-time activities and were often to be found in Reading Gaol. Born to an itinerant way of life, the barge people had little opportunity for formal education. Their illiteracy and their scanty knowledge of the Scriptures caused the Rev. Field to comment that 'this degraded class of our fellow operatives' were deprived of the privileges afforded to others on the Sabbath and were thereby led astray. The locks below Staines were in fact closed on Sundays between the hours of 10 a.m. and 5 p.m. in order to bring the river traffic to a standstill. To the bargees, however, time was money and those engaged on upstream journies would make the earliest possible start on Sunday in order to pass Staines lock before it closed and would continue to work throughout the day.

Ascot races would bring its annual crop of petty offenders who, having been dealt with by the Magistrates' Court on the racecourse, would be brought to Reading by train for admission to prison. In 1868, no fewer than 32 prisoners were received from Ascot, the majority convicted of loitering with intent to pick pockets. From this time until 1914, the number of offenders sent to prison for offences committed on the racecourse averaged 40 per meeting.

Throughout the course of the nineteenth century and well into the twentieth, imprisonment was regarded as the general antidote for social misconduct. It was therefore inevitable that the bulk of the prison population should be made up from the ranks of those persons unfitted to look after themselves in a free society – pilferers, vagrants, drunkards and inadequates from the casual labouring and near-unemployable classes. It has indeed been calculated that over 80 per cent of committals were in respect of misbehaviour that was essentially non-criminal – drunkenness, gaming, wandering without visible means of support, breach of workhouse rules and of local by-laws. The majority of the sentences imposed were of short duration, about one half of these were of fourteen days or less. Less than 1 per cent were of one year or over.

The following represents receptions into the prison during the course of one week in October, 1910:

S. Scott (57)	Lodge in shed	7 days H.L.
T. Akerman (39)	,, ,, ,,	7 days H.L.
J. Doyle (60)	Begging	14 days H.L.
R. Davis (50)	Steal tea caddy	3 months H.L.
J. Knock (21)	Refuse workhouse task	7 days H.L.
T. Gibbons (19)	Attempt carnal knowledge	2 months H.L.
H. Whurr (40)	Larceny	3 months H.L.
E. College (37)	Burglary	3 months H.L.
J. Burke (53)	Steal boots	6 weeks
J. Keating (32)	False pretences	9 months H.L.
A. Chandler (19)	Indecent assault	3 months H.L.

The authorities were not completely blind to the futility of the short sentences of imprisonment all too frequently imposed upon inadequate, petty offenders but unfortunately there were few alternatives open to the sentencing Magistrates. In 1907, the members of the Visiting Committee of Reading Prison expressed their agreement with their fellow Justices of Lancaster Prison whom they supported in their representations to the Home Secretary concerning the undesirability of committing 'weak-minded, mentally defective and physically helpless prisoners of the inebriate and vagrant classes' and suggesting a Disciplinary Home – an institution midway between a prison and a workhouse – as more appropriate to meet such cases. These representations fell upon stony soil and to the present day there is no adequate provision for the persistent petty offender, the person who appears day after day before the Magistrates' Court charged with being drunk in a public place and for the vagrant who prefers to 'skipper' (sleep in derelict buildings) rather than accept more salubrious lodgings.

Youth did not exempt the juvenile offender from committal to prison. In June, 1845, we see George James and Stephen Knight of Thatcham, lads barely into their teens being sent to imprisonment with hard labour for 12 months with an order that they be privately whipped on discharge. Their crime was that of taking two cricket bats, two boys' caps and a pocket knife valued at 1d. from some younger children. The sentence was harsh as both had previously been before the Court, James having been imprisoned in December, 1844, for 14 days for stealing a quantity of rope.

Half a century later young children were still being sent to prison as witnessed by the following entries from the Admission Register of 1892/3:

19 Aug. 1891	J .Watts (14)	Throwing stones	3 days impt.
26 Sept. 1891	W. Watts (10)	Steal cherries	3 days H.L.
9 Feb. 1892	A. Davis (11)	Steal rabbit	21 days H.L. and 12 strokes of birch
10 May 1892	Prudence Ford (14)	Steal 3 pairs of boots	10 days impt.
1 July 1892	Ada Smith (14)	Steal pair of shoes	14 days H.L.

Prison was certainly no deterrent to John Watts, the subject of the first of the above entries as he was again sent to prison for 14 days in January 1892 convicted of stealing 1 lb. of sweets, for 14 days in April for throwing stones and in September for a further 14 days, this time with hard labour, for stealing fruit. He had not been at liberty for more than two days following his release from the latter sentence when he was brought before the Reading Borough Magistrates and sent back for a further 5 days for trespassing on the railway.

The younger offender who in the view of the Court required training away from home could be ordered to one or other of the Industrial or Reformatory Schools. Such action had however to be preceeded by a term of imprisonment:

10 June 1891	Thomas Boddington (12). Steal zinc pipe. 10 days H.L. then 4 years reformatory school. Removed to Royal Philanthropic Society's School, Redhill.
8 Sept. 1891	Jim James (13). Steal money. 14 days Impt then 3 years at reformatory school. To Warminster School.
1 Feb. 1892	Bertie Lane (11). Steal money. 14 days impt then 5 years at Reformatory School. To Redhill.
9 Feb. 1892	George Loader. Steal rabbit. 21 days H.L. then 3 yrs at Reformatory School.

Of all the prisoners, those whose lot was the least to be envied were the unfortunates upon whom sentence of death had been passed. Until well into the nineteenth century, the death sentence was mandatory following conviction for certain offences and the entry 'Death recorded' appears against many names in the Assize Calendars of the period. Fortunately, the capital sentence was not invariably put into effect. Until 1861, the Judge himself had the power to commute the sentence, a privilege of which he would often avail himself. Where the Court did not order a respite, the sentence would be reviewed by the Sovereign and the Privy Council. Known as the 'Hanging Cabinet', it was at these meetings that petitions for clemency and recommendations to mercy were studied. This procedure was abandoned in

1837 upon the accession to the Throne of Queen Victoria, it being rightly felt that Her Majesty who was then only 18 years of age was too young and of the wrong sex to discuss with her Ministers particulars of crimes, some of which were hideous in the extreme. From this time onwards the power of life and death was vested in the Home Secretary.

Until 1868, executions were carried out in public. Whilst it was intended that the spectacle should serve as a salutory lesson to the onlookers, the reality was altogether different. A hanging provided something akin to an entertainment to the curious, the vicious and the idle. Writing in 1888, W. S. Darter, J.P. who had himself witnessed several public executions in Reading comments: 'Women respectably dressed, some with children in their arms formed a large element of the crowds, whose spirit of levity and brutality stung more and more the conscience of the community.' A crowd of 5,000 assembled to see John Carter hanged in 1833 and no less than 10,000, of whom a great proportion were women, gathered to witness the execution of Thomas Jennings in 1844, the first to be carried out at the new gaol.

Until the opening of the gaol in Forbury Road, executions were carried out at a spot in Lower Earley known locally as 'No Man's Land' or 'Gallows Tree Common'. On these occasions the condemned would be conveyed from the County Gaol in an open cart which would stop by custom at the Oxford Arms public-house in Sivier (Silver) Street where the prisoner and the hangman would take a drink together. The body of the hanged prisoner would, unless claimed by his friends or relatives, be brought back for burial in St Mary's churchyard.

The old County Gaol in Forbury Road was equipped with the newly invented drop apparatus which would be erected on the roof at the western end of the building as required. The siting took account of a small paddock, now the site of St James's Roman Catholic Church, in which spectators could assemble.

By an Act of Parliament of 1752 'For Better Preventing the Horrid Crime of Murder' it was laid down that persons convicted of murder should be executed within 48 hours of sentence. In the interim the condemned was to receive a diet of bread and water. The sentence in respect of other capital offences would be carried into effect in about a fortnight.

A list of all executions carried out at the County Gaol since 1800 is given in Appendix II. Of the 25 men hanged at the old gaol only 9 had taken life; the remainder, with the exception of one who had committed an offence of an unnatural nature, had been found guilty of offences against property or in connection with the forgery of cheques or banknotes.

One of the youngest men to be hanged here was George King aged 19 years. An agricultural labourer of hitherto good character, King went into 'The White Hart' inn at Wantage where he asked to be accommodated for the night. The last customers having departed, the landlady, Mrs Pullen, served him with a meal. Having eaten, King attacked Mrs Pullen with a bean hook and with one blow severed her head. His motive appears to have been one of robbery but his gains amounted to only fourteen shillings and a few pence. When arrested he was found to have in his possession a crooked sixpence which the landlady kept in the bottom of her purse as a lucky charm. Whilst King's prime motive was robbery, one suspects that this man may have been the victim of mental disturbance as *post mortem* examination of his body revealed a fissure in his skull measuring some five inches by three quarters, the result of an injury sustained some years previously in a fall from a hay loft. After dissection and the taking of a plaster cast of the face, the body is reported to have been 'placed in a hole in one of the spare wards without the least ceremony'.

One of the few murders to be committed in Reading was that by William Spicer, a basket-maker of 16, Howard Street, of his wife. It would seem that Mrs Spicer who was renowned for the sharpness of her tongue finally drove her husband beyond endurance causing him to batter her to death with a poker. Realizing what he had done, Spicer threw the body down the cellar steps and contrived to create the appearance of an accident.

At his trial in March, 1835, before Baron Platt some 30 witnesses were called. Despite the length of the hearing, the Jury was absent for only ten minutes before bringing in a verdict of 'guilty'. The execution which took place at noon on 20 March 1835, the last to be carried out at the old gaol, was witnessed by some 5,000 people.

In building the new gaol, the architect had thoughtfully provided the Gate Lodge with a flat roof upon which executions might be staged. The public did not have long to wait before it was used for this purpose. On 22 March 1844, protesting his innocence to the very end, Thomas Jennings was hanged for the murder of his son, Eleazar, aged 4 years. It was alleged that Jennings placed a saucer of white arsenic near the child's place at dinner. Eleazar, mistaking the substance for salt, dipped his food into it and was within a short time taken mortally ill. It was not until another member of the family was found to be suffering from arsenical poisoning that the child's body was exhumed. Poison being present in the remains, Jennings was tried and convicted of murder.

Twenty-two years were to pass before the next spectacle. The principal actor in this tragedy was John Gould, aged 39 years, of Windsor, who was brought before the Lent Assizes of 1862, charged with the murder of his daughter, Hannah. It was alleged that Gould arriving home in a drunken state found that his seven-years-old daughter had not carried out his instructions to clean the house. Saying that he would teach her a lesson, he deliberately cut her throat with a razor causing her to bleed quickly to death. Despite the nature of his offence and his previous record of violent behaviour there was public support for a reprieve and a petition bearing 300 signatures was presented to the Home Secretary. On the day prior to that fixed for the execution a deputation led by the Mayor of Reading was received by the Home Secretary. The law was however to take its course and the *Berkshire Chronicle* of 15 March 1862, reporting the events of the previous day relates that 'from the early morning the roads to the town were lined by those who had come to see the ceremony. . . . Hours before the time fixed many persons had congregated before the spot in order to take up a good position.' So dense were the crowds that barriers had to be set up in Forbury Road to keep the space before the gaol clear. Those spectators who could not find a suitable spot in the meadow opposite the gaol climbed upon the railway embankment.

At 12 noon, the Under-Sheriff, Mr Blandy, went to the condemned cell to receive the prisoner from the Governor, Mr Ferry. The procession to the scaffold was led by the Chaplain wearing his surplice. There followed the condemned man escorted by two Warders, the Governor, the Under-Sheriff, the Deputy Governor, the Public Executioner, Calcraft, and other officers of the gaol. Gould is said to have walked with a firm step to the gallows where the execution took place with the minimum of delay. The body was left to hang in full view of the public for an hour before being taken down for burial in an unmarked plot under the boundary wall.

All subsequent executions were carried out in private within the gaol. The first of these was the double hanging of the brothers, Henry and Francis Tidbury, convicted at the Berkshire Assizes of January, 1877, of the violent murder of two police officers. Upon challenging the men whom he suspected of poaching, P.C. Drewitt was shot dead. Inspector Shorter who came to his aid was battered to death with the butt of the gun. Francis, who when arrested stated that he was 16 years of age (it was believed that he was, in fact, 18 or 19) was recommended by the Jury to clemency. Representations were made on his behalf by several clergymen and a few members of the medical and legal profession. These together with a petition bearing 1,000 signatures were received by the Home Secretary, but without avail. On this occasion members of the Press were permitted to be present at the execution and a full account of the proceedings appears in the *Reading Mercury* of Saturday, 17 March 1877. After this time attendance was limited to the Under-Sheriff, officers of the gaol and to any Justices of the

Peace who cared to be present. The Press was strictly excluded. Crowds still congregated before the gate to await the hoisting of the black flag which indicated that the sentence had been carried out and the atmosphere was made tense by the tolling of the bell of St Laurence's Church.

The hanging on Tuesday, 7 July 1896, of Charles Thomas Wooldridge, a Trooper of Horse Guards, for the murder at Clewer near Windsor of his wife is immortalized by Oscar Wilde in 'The Ballad of Reading Gaol'. The crime was in reality a sordid, domestic affair, the wife having rejected her husband in favour of another man. In this case, too, strong representations were made to the Home Secretary drawing his attention to certain mitigating factors and emphasizing the strong recommendation to mercy which accompanied the verdict of the Jury. A petition for clemency was circulated in Reading and about a thousand signatures obtained. Another petition was forwarded from Wooldridge's home village of East Garston. The authorities were however of the view that the crime was premeditated – why else, they asked, should the man have gone out of his way to carry a cut-throat razor when calling upon his estranged wife? There was no reprieve and the sentence was carried out according to law.

The last execution to take place at Reading Gaol was in February, 1913, when Eric Sedgwick a house porter at Eton College paid with his life for the murder of a young woman. Sedgwick was not the only man to be sentenced by the Buckinghamshire Assizes of the previous month. Also condemned was Philip Trueman, convicted of murdering his girl friend at Bourne End. For a fortnight Trueman and Sedgwick occupied adjacent cells in the condemned suite and it was arranged that both should die on Tuesday 4 February. At the eleventh hour Trueman was granted a reprieve on the grounds that his crime was not premeditated and the sentence was commuted to that of Penal Servitude for life.

Of all the prisoners who have served their sentence at Reading, by far and away the most well known is Oscar Wilde, poet, dramatist, philosopher and wit.

Following his unsuccessful libel action against the Marquis of Queensbury, Wilde was himself indicted under the Criminal Law Amendment Act, 1887. The trial opened at the Old Bailey before Mr Justice Charles on 26 April 1895, and lasted for five days, Wilde pleading 'Not guilty' to the charges of gross indecency levelled against him. The jury found itself unable to agree upon a verdict, was discharged and a new trial ordered.

The second trial, again at the Old Bailey but before Mr Justice Henwick Wills, commenced on 20 May. In the afternoon of Saturday 25 May, the jury retired to return after two hours' deliberation with a verdict of 'Guilty'. In addressing Wilde and his codefendant Alfred Taylor, the Judge who had shown little sympathy for either accused throughout the trial informed them that he would be expected to pass the severest sentence that the law allowed. 'In my judgment,' he went on to say, 'it is totally inadequate for such a case as this. The sentence of the Court is that each of you be imprisoned and kept to hard labour for two years.'

It being Saturday, Wilde was detained for the weekend in Newgate Gaol which at that time adjoined the Old Bailey. On Monday morning he was conveyed to Pentonville where he experienced all the humiliation of the reception procedure and was initiated into the routine of prison life of the Du Cane era with its endless privations and restrictions. Certified as fit only for 'light labour', Wilde was excused work at the treadwheel or the crank and was put to the no less unattractive tasks of picking oakum and sewing mail bags in solitary confinement. To a person of Wilde's sensitivity, particularly to one who had enjoyed as affluent a life as he, the experience was one of profound shock. The poor and scanty diet, the discomfort of the plank bed and above all the enforced silence and segregation reduced him to a state of abject misery.

In July 1895, Wilde was transferred from Pentonville to Wandsworth where he found conditions even less congenial than at the former establishment. He became increasingly depressed and his physical condition deteriorated. It was indeed rumoured in the popular press that he was suffering a serious mental breakdown. The prison authorities duly called for a medical assessment and he was examined by two doctors from Broadmoor Hospital. Although he was found by them to be of sound mind, it was recommended, *inter alia*, that he should be transferred to some suitable country prison. The machinery of the Prison Commission creaked slowly into action and on 13 November 1895, Wilde was conveyed to Reading where he was to spend the remainder of his sentence.

Before he was transferred, Wilde was obliged to suffer the further public indignity of an appearance in the Bankruptcy Court following a petition by Queensbury requesting that a Receiving Order be made. The sum claimed was £677 being the taxed costs of the defendant in the abortive criminal libel action.

Upon his arrival at Reading Prison, Wilde was allocated to cell no. 3 on the third landing of C Wing. For prison purposes he was known as C3.3. and it was under this pseudonym that 'The Ballad of Reading Gaol' was originally published.

Life at Reading Gaol was no more acceptable than that at the great London prisons. The Governor at that time was Lieut-Col. Henry Isaacson, an unimaginative administrator noted for the frequency with which he would award quite severe punishment for even minor breaches of prison discipline. Avowed that he would 'knock the nonsense out of Oscar Wilde' his favourite punishment was to deprive his distinguished inmate of the books which he valued so greatly. In the years following his release, Wilde was scathing in his comments concerning the Governor: 'harsh and stupid', 'lacking in imagination' and in a letter to the publishers of 'The Ballad of Reading Gaol' he refers to him as 'a mulberry faced Dictator, a great red-faced, bloated Jew, who always looked as though he drank, and did so. . . . Brandy was the flaming message of his pulpy face.' He was critical, too, of the Medical Officer, Dr Oliver Morris, and of the Chaplain, the Rev. M. T. Friend, whom he describes, uncharitably, as 'a good natured fool, one of the silliest of God's sheep, a typical clergyman in fact'.

Wilde was treated in a callous manner by some of the members of the staff. A few of the Warders were however more friendly towards him and he responded to them with warmth. It is said that he employed his literary abilities in assisting them with their entries in newspaper competitions and was successful in winning a silver tea service for one of them and a grand piano for another.

He appears to have established a particularly good relationship with Warder Tom Martin who for a while had charge of C3 landing. Martin frequently broke the prison rules and supplied Wilde with items of food including such delicacies as white bread and ginger biscuits. He also brought newspapers and magazines. Shortly after Wilde's release, this officer was dismissed the service having been discovered handing biscuits which he had bought for his own consumption to some small boys newly committed to prison. In support of Martin, Wilde wrote a letter of protest which was published in the *Daily Chronicle* of 28 May 1897. Under the heading 'The Case of Warder Martin: Some Cruelties of Prison Life' Wilde not only complained of the Warder's dismissal for what was nothing more than an act of kindness but spoke out against the undesirability of sending young children to prison in the first place.

This together with a further letter published in the same newspaper in March, 1898, exposing the negative aspects of imprisonment proved a powerful weapon in the hands of the prison reformers of the day and it is regretted that Wilde did not follow their suggestion and write a more lengthy work on prison reform.

Wilde appears to have got on well with his fellow prisoners in whom he took a keen interest and with whom he soon learned to communicate, although not so efficiently as to go completely undetected. In his earlier letter to the *Daily Chronicle* he says of them:

> Their cheerfulness under terrible circumstances, their sympathy for each other, their humility, their gentleness, their pleasant smiles of greeting when they meet each other, their complete acquiescence in their punishments, are all quite wonderful, and I myself learned many lessons from them.

Following his release he wrote to a number of them sending small sums of money from his own limited resources. One discharged prisoner, a former soldier, he invited to spend a weekend with him at Berneval-sur-Mer and was pleasantly surprised when he actually turned up.

Having spent some fourteen months in prison during which time his health deteriorated and he lived in constant fear of going out of his mind, Wilde availed himself of his right to petition the Home Secretary requesting that he be considered for an early release from prison on medical grounds. Not only did he fear insanity but he was genuinely alarmed lest he lose both his sight and hearing. Unfortunately for him his petition was so well reasoned in its argument that it failed completely in its purpose. The matter was however referred to the Visiting Committee who reported that in their opinion they did not consider that the prisoner was in any danger of becoming insane. It was however, recommended that a special medical examination be undertaken with particular attention being paid to the state of his eyesight and hearing. It was noted that Wilde himself had stated that his treatment had been good and the food adequate for his needs, that he had been relieved of oakum picking and allowed more books and exercise than the other prisoners. The papers were duly referred to Dr Nicholson of Broadmoor, one of the doctors who had examined Wilde the previous year. He did not advise any further investigation of Wilde's mental condition and there the matter appears to have rested. The Governor was however directed by the Home Secretary to permit Wilde the use of pen, ink and paper for use in his leisure time and to ensure that he had access to sufficient books to occupy his mind.

By the end of July 1896 Lieut-Col Isaacson was transferred and his place taken by Major J. B. Nelson, a younger man of more liberal and humane views, with whom Wilde was to become quite friendly.

Despite the rejection of a further petition to the Home Secretary requesting that his sentence be commuted, Wilde's final months of imprisonment were comparatively uneventful. He appears to have been excused most forms of manual labour and was appointed 'Schoolmaster's Orderly'. His duties brought him into contact with the prison library, a small collection of books mainly of a religious and improving kind. Apalled by their dull sterility he arranged for a dozen or so volumes to be sent in at his own expense.

With his newly won writing materials he commenced a lengthy letter to his friend, Lord Alfred Douglas ('Bosie'), parts of which were to be published after his death by his literary executor, Robert Ross, under the title *De Profundis*. This work which is regarded by many as his finest masterpiece was written mostly in the evenings by dim gaslight on a table improvised from his plank bed. As each sheet of ruled prison paper was completed it was handed to the Governor and another issued in its place. The Prison Commissioners, whilst not permitting the completed work to be sent out during the currency of Wilde's sentence, gave a direction that it should be kept and handed to him upon discharge.

As the day of his discharge drew near, Wilde became increasingly alarmed at the possibility of unwelcome publicity, a fear matched by his apprehension lest the Marquis of Queensbury and his prize-fighting friends also pursue him. Appeals to the Home Secretary for an early release met with a negative response. It was however arranged that he should be taken on the eve of his release to Pentonville from whence he might be discharged to the care of his friends at a mutually convenient time.

Late in the evening of Tuesday 18 May 1897, Wilde dressed in the clothes which he had last worn at the Old Bailey, was taken in a closed cab to Twyford Station where, escorted by the Chief Warder, he was placed aboard the London train. Despite these precautions, two newspaper reporters were waiting outside the gaol at the time of his departure. The party did not however go on to Paddington where a reception committee of the Press was almost certain to await, but alighted at Westbourne Park and completed the journey to Pentonville by cab. The following morning Wilde boarded a carriage hired by his friends and drove off some twenty minutes before the hour at which discharges usually took place. Later, following a reunion with a number of his closer friends, he left for France never again to set foot in England.

After a brief stay in Dieppe, Wilde settled in a small hotel at Berneval-sur-Mer. It was here and not, as popularly believed, in prison that his best known poetic work, 'The Ballad of Reading Gaol' was written. The idea had come to him when in the spring of 1896 he noticed among the remand prisoners at Reading a young man, a Trooper in the Royal Horse Guards, by the name of Charles Thomas Wooldridge who it was alleged had murdered his wife. In reality this was a rather sordid domestic murder in which the husband, driven to distraction by his wife's infidelity, cut her throat with a razor. Tried before Mr Justice Hawkins at the Berkshire Assizes he was found guilty, sentenced to death and hanged on 7 July 1896. In simple but vivid language the poet tells of the impact of the execution upon the inmates of the gaol. 'The Ballad' is dedicated to the memory of the executed Trooper who is described only by his initials. Wilde likewise veils his own identity in the anonymity of his cell number, C3.3.

9 ESCAPE

As stated in an earlier chapter, the primary function of the prison is to contain those persons whose removal from the community has been ordered by the operation of the Law. The prisoner population does not however take kindly to being locked up – particularly in the grey, uncomfortable environment of a penal institution. Whilst the majority of prisoners are able sooner or later to come to terms with their situation there are some who are subject to overpowering burdens of worry concerning homes and families left behind, some stand in fear of the criminal fraternity with whom they are obliged to live, yet others are overwhelmed by feelings of frustration and burning resentment, forces which can drive one to violence, insanity, suicide or – escape. To a few unfortunates like Charles White, escape may offer the only way of preserving one's life.

Among the younger prisoners, he who makes a successful break is often regarded as a hero by his fellows. He may complain that various atrocities experienced in the institution have caused him to make the break but his underlying motivation can usually be traced to a need for adulation. The older prisoner will, as a general rule, have a greater regard for the long-term consequences of running away and will take into his calculations the likelihood of severe punishment upon recapture and the certainty that the remainder of his stay in prison will be less comfortable than previously. He may wish a fellow prisoner well in an escape bid but will privately consider that he should have his head examined.

To the authorities and to the public alike, an escape is an open admission that the prison has fallen down on the job. To a prison governor the escaped prisoner is an embarrassment as a result of whose inconsiderate behaviour reports must be made, questions answered and blame apportioned. To the less informed element of the public, the prisoner is seen as a desperate individual who will stop at nothing and an escaped prisoner as doubly dangerous. The general public enjoys nothing so much as a manhunt and press reports relating to escapes from prison are for this reason usually quite full and informative. Particulars of attempted escapes are on the other hand less readily available as the authorities in their aversion to negative publicity tend to cover such occurrences in various ways. An attempt to cut through a prison wall, for instance, would in all probability be reported and dealt with as wilful damage to prison property; a prisoner concealing himself in some part of the building to await an opportunity to slip away is more likely to be reported for being absent from his place of work.

The haphazard construction of the old Reading gaol, the overcrowding, the inadequate staffing and the generally depressing surroundings provided the precipitating factor in many of the escapes, some of which were completely successful, which took place during the first 40 years of the nineteenth century. If an escaper were able to leave the town before the hue and cry were raised, the rudimentary communications of those times allowed him a sporting chance of retaining his liberty. There being no photographs available, his description would be given in writing and circulated by messenger to his home parish and to the Peace Officers of the surrounding towns. It was also the custom of the Keeper to insert advertisements in the county and local Press describing the absentee and offering a reward for his recapture.

Once at liberty the escaper must have food, shelter and proper clothing if he is to live honestly. Having regard to his circumstances these necessities would be very hard to come by in the normal way, with the result that he would be compelled to take his chance in criminal haunts where he was almost certain to become involved in further unlawful activity. Many of the prisoners who escaped from the old gaol are next heard of when apprehended elsewhere for further offences.

An early attempt at escape is recorded in the Minute Books of the Berkshire Quarter Sessions of Michaelmas 1799. In August of that year we read of Benjamin Josey and William Hutchins being brought before the Court to answer for an attempt to escape by tunnelling through the floor of their sleeping quarters. It was not only escape that they had in mind. Over a period of time they had accumulated matches and a quantity of tinder with the intention of burning the hated building down. It was their fire-raising plans that led to their downfall as a fellow prisoner, realizing the loss of life that would almost certainly have resulted, reported the matter to the gaoler. The Justices took a serious view of the matter and ordered that both men should be kept in irons for the remainder of their sentence and that Josey, whom they considered to be the ringleader, should further be kept in solitary confinement.

Another unsuccessful escaper was Charles White. Already notorious for their thieving propensities, White and his sons Thomas and James were committed in custody to Reading Gaol in July 1811, suspected of horse stealing. They were well aware that in the event of an unfavourable verdict they were likely to face a capital sentence or, at the very least, transportation for life. Determined to save his life and liberty, White soon formed a plan to secure his own freedom and that of anyone wishing to join with him. The essence of the plot was that they should break into the Keeper's house, kill him and seize his keys. White and a band of half a dozen or so followers did indeed force an entry into the house where they encountered Mrs Knight, the Keeper's wife, whom they took as a hostage and locked in the condemned cell. One can only assume that the lady did not submit without protest as the Keeper who was in another part of the prison at the time heard the commotion and arming himself with a brace of pistols confronted the conspirators who were making their way to the front gate and freedom.

Undismayed by failure, White proceeded to hatch another plot to escape and to revenge himself upon the Keeper in the process. His plan was for the prisoners to riot whilst assembled in the chapel and to kill both the Keeper and the Chaplain. The enormity of the suggestion was however too great for the majority of the prisoners and word was discretely passed to the Keeper who was able to isolate the ringleaders. Ironically, White when brought before the Court was found by the Grand Jury to have no case to answer and was discharged. He did not however profit by the experience and barely a year later was indicted on further charges of horse stealing. Found guilty, he was sentenced to death and hanged at Reading on 26 March 1814 before a large crowd.

A rising whilst the prisoners were together in the chapel was again plotted in 1831. At this time the gaol was filled to overflowing with men sentenced for their part in the agricultural riots which had swept the rural areas. Angry men who considered themselves victims of political repression and by no means common criminals, they planned to overpower the turnkeys and to break out *en masse*. On this occasion the Keeper was forewarned by a prisoner, William Appleby. Serving a two-year sentence for horse stealing and considering himself a good, honest crook, Appleby seems to have had little sympathy for the argumentative interlopers. The dangers which could arise from a disturbance in the chapel having been pointed out, steps were taken to strengthen the pews whilst the internal railings were fitted with spikes. Appleby was rewarded for his services by recommendation for Royal mercy and was shortly after released.

In October, 1802, an unnamed prisoner is reported to have made his escape by scaling the south boundary wall, some 20 ft high. It may be assumed that he managed to cut through the bolt of his cell door as it was subsequently ordered that the existing bolts should be replaced by a more substantial fitting of case-hardened steel. Further, metal guard plates 'to prevent a saw getting at the bolt' were fitted to the inner side of the doors.

It was further ordered that estimates for the cost of a pointed fence of wood or iron to surmount the wall be obtained. This work was not however carried out.

In October, 1828, John Tiley, a prisoner sentenced to a term of 14 years, having suffered ill health was permitted by the Surgeon to live under conditions of relaxed security and was able to move unsupervised about the establishment. Suspicion being allayed, he was able to evade the Turnkey and walk unmolested into Reading. Another prisoner who was allowed to move freely about the premises was a man named Williams who in 1833 was sentenced to 2 years' imprisonment with hard labour. Unfit for employment on the treadmill he was appointed gardener and employed in Mr Eastaff's extensive ornamental garden. Williams did not escape but was discovered to be in the habit of slipping away to the nearest ale house, often returning intoxicated. His services as gardener came to an end when he was discovered in the act of returning the gaoler's horse to its stable having taken it for an unauthorized ride.

Negligence on the part of Turnkey, Thomas Webb, contributed to the escape in June 1832, of Henry Mullis, a deserter from the Royal Horse Artillery temporarily detained in the House of Correction pending the arrival of a military escort to take him back to his regiment. The prisoners having been unlocked and ordered to Chapel, Mullis remained in his cell. When all was quiet, using his wooden bedstead as a ladder, he climbed on to the flat roof from whence he descended by way of a scaffold pole left by the builders then engaged in the construction of the juvenile prison. There is no record of his ever having been apprehended. Thomas Webb for his part was summoned before Quarter Sessions and publicly reprimanded.

A few weeks earlier, John Dickinson, a man who had unlawfully returned from a sentence of Transportation, in itself a capital offence, and who was subsequently convicted and sentenced to death for burglary, made good his escape by cutting through the 2-in. oak planks of the ceiling of his cell. A difficult enough task employing proper carpenter's tools,

Dickinson's only implement was an improvised saw made from a piece of jagged iron barrel hoop inserted into a stick. Progress was painfully slow and the task occupied several nights. At daybreak he concealed the cut by means of strips of paper stuck on by paste made from bread and water, the whole being camouflaged with whitewash scraped from the walls of the cell and mixed with water. Free from his cell, Dickinson made his way across the flat roofs and lowered himself to the garden by way of a rope of plaited strips of bed ticking.

In the course of the enquiry into the escape it was revealed that whereas the ceilings and walls of the more modern parts of the building were sheathed in iron to prevent such an escape, this precaution had never been taken in the older area of the gaol. Dickinson was next heard of some three months later at Warwick where he was tried and sentenced for further offences. In the meanwhile, the cell from which he had escaped together with the one adjoining had been strengthened with iron plates to frustrate further potential escapers.

In July 1839, four prisoners convicted of offences of burglary and sentenced to varying terms of imprisonment were temporarily confined in the condemned cell there being no room in any of the other male wards. Their temporary quarters should by right have been the most secure in the gaol. Described by the Governor as 'lynx-eyed', they observed that the lintel of the doorway had been fashioned from an ill-fitting piece of wood to which a plank some 6 ft in length and 4 in. breadth had been fastened to conceal the gap. This item being but lightly tacked was detached without difficulty to provide the prisoners with a lever by means of which they were able to force the bars of the window. Once through the window they made a perilous exit along the top of a wall, the upper brickwork of which was crumbling and in danger of imminent collapse. This escape and that of Jabez Blake in September, 1840, caused the Visiting Justices to express the view that the whole of the interior of the building stood in need of complete reconstruction.

On the way to Abingdon Bridewell whence the inmates were

transferred following the closure of the gaol in 1842 for re-building, one man is reported to have slipped his handcuffs and to have made his escape by throwing himself from the coach in which a group of prisoners were being conveyed.

In designing the new gaol the architects had security in mind. Both within the building and without, visibility was good. There were few blind spots in which an inmate might conceal himself and no physical connection between the main building and the boundary walls. The Separate System under which the gaol was designed to operate required that no prisoner should move from his cell unescorted. The system permitted of the minimum of association between prisoners with the result that conspiracy was virtually impossible. Escapes from this building have been very few in number. One suspects however that the price of enhanced security was reflected in the high rate of mental illness observed among the prisoners during the latter half of the nineteenth century.

Escape attempts, unless the circumstances were blatantly obvious, are generally unrecorded and it is unfortunately not possible to ascertain their number over the past hundred years. We do however know that in November 1887, Henry Marchant was punished with 14 days' cellular confinement for attempting to remove bricks from the wall of his cell with a view to escape. A month later, Thomas Jones was rather more successful in that he was able to make his way out of the building. He was how-ever spotted on the top of the wall of the Debtors' airing yard and brought back. In his possession was a knotted cord to which he had attached a bag of stones. Using this as a grapnel he had hoped to scale the boundary wall.

On the morning of 2 May 1879, a female prisoner named Esther Chamberlain was found to be missing from her cell in E Wing. It was apparent that she had left her cell having slipped the bolt of the lock but how she managed to make her escape from the locked Wing and over the boundary wall was never discovered. So far as is known she had no facsimile keys neither had she the benefit of outside help. After eight days at liberty she was recognized and arrested by a Constable of the Oxfordshire Constabulary at Goring on Thames and returned to prison.

The cell locks which were installed in 1844 were remarkably efficient and many remained in use until 1968. Very few prisoners were able to pick these but on a July evening in 1906, at a time when the inmates had been locked away for the night, a prisoner by the name of Bird was observed by a Warder to be looking out from the open door of his cell. Brought before the Visiting Justices to answer to the allegation that he was trying to escape Bird indignantly denied the charge. Whilst admitting that he had indeed looked out from his cell, he explained that the door was not in fact properly secured. Unknown to Bird, the Chief Warder, a long serving officer well versed in all the tricks employed by prisoners, had himself looked in that cell. With the aid of a knife he quickly had the door open. Having heard this evidence, the Visiting Justices found the charge proved and could then be informed that, whilst at Wormwood Scrubs during the previous year this man had twice attempted similar acts. The penalty in this case was an order for 7 days' close confinement together with a forfeiture of remission marks.

There were a few escapes during the First World War when the prison was employed as a place of internment for enemy aliens and Irish detainees. It is however strange to relate that it was not until 1918 that the Defence Regulations were amended to make escape a punishable offence. Among the aliens who escaped and evaded recapture was a Belgian, Louis Claas, who slipped away in November 1916. For over a year nothing was heard of him. At Christmas 1917, this man who whilst in detention had expressed the strongest pro-German sentiments, presented himself at the prison wearing the uniform of a Private in the British Army stating that he had enlisted in the 13th Battalion of the Middlesex Regiment then stationed at Reading. The Governor in his Journal remarks that whilst Claas gave the reason for this visit as an enquiry concerning property that he had left behind, it was suspected that he had really come in the hope of seeing some of his old friends. He was not admitted to the prison.

Four more internees were able to escape in 1917 having manufactured a key with which they were able to open the gate of the exercise yard. Two were arrested and returned the same night but the others do not appear to have been traced.

A few young men escaped during the years that the premises were used as a Borstal Recall Centre. The majority of these appear to have absconded from outside working parties but three did it the hard way, making what was perhaps the most daring escape in the history of the prison. Climbing to the roof trusses of the chapel by way of the rod which operates the clerestory windows, they made their way on to the roof of D Wing. Descending to the yard by means of the rainwater pipes they scaled the outer wall using only a broom. At any stage of this perilous journey a slip would have meant death or, at the very least, serious injury.

If prizes were to be awarded for ingenuity, the outright winner would have been a lad by the name of Johnson who, having secreted himself in the gymnasium, unscrewed the bars guarding one of the windows. He then scaled the boundary wall using a ladder which he had improvised from items of gymnastic apparatus and descended into the Forbury Gardens by means of a climbing rope which he had brought for that purpose. He was at liberty for but two days, his freedom coming to an end when his hiding place in a barn near Basingstoke was discovered by the farmer's dog.

The most recent escape took place in December, 1969, when a prisoner serving a sentence of 12 months climbed an internal fence to reach the top of the boundary wall. Seen to drop into Forbury Road he disappeared into the rush-hour traffic. Road blocks were set up around the town and vehicles searched but to no avail. He was recaptured the following day in London about a mile from his home. Upon his return to Reading he was brought before the Board of Visitors which ordered the forfeiture of the greater part of the remission which under normal circumstances he would have earned for good conduct.

10 H.M. PLACE OF INTERNMENT

August Bank Holiday, 1914. After a fortnight of uncertainty, war spread across Europe like an epidemic. On all sides an upsurge of patriotic feeling was accompanied by a corresponding wave of xenophobia and spy mania. By the time war was formally declared almost all foreign holiday-makers and the majority of the nationals of those countries which were now in opposition to the Allies had departed. Those who were stranded or had chosen to remain were obliged to register with the Police, many being interned forthwith. Also taken into custody were nationals of neutral and even of friendly countries who were suspected of having anti-British sympathies. By the spring of 1915 there were some 19,000 aliens in internment, some of whom had been taken to large camps such as that established at Alexandra Palace. A great many were on the other hand taking up valuable space in local prisons throughout the country.

During the early years of the war, due to the demands of the armed forces for recruits and the abundance of employment throughout the country, there was a decline in the numbers committed to prison if not in the actual crime rate. By November 1915, the inmate population of Reading prison had fallen to a mere 71. The Prison Commissioners accordingly directed the removal of the civilian prisoners and having consulted the Visiting Committee, an act of courtesy as the Justices had little if any power to resist the decision, redesignated the establishment 'H.M. Place of Internment'. Within a few weeks there were some 68 male aliens in residence, the majority of whom were transferred from the camp at Alexandra Palace and from Brixton Prison.

Whilst it was imperative that a degree of law and order be maintained, the regime was not that of a penal establishment. Within the secure perimeter of the prison, the inmates were allowed a reasonable degree of freedom. In the interests of National security their correspondence both incoming and outgoing was subject to careful scrutiny whilst visits were strictly supervised. Not only had the Officer in charge of the visiting room to assure himself that the conversation between the internee and his visitor was confined to domestic and business matters, he was afterwards obliged to submit a summary to the Governor.

The internee community was multi-national and multilingual. Whilst the majority of inmates were of German origin, men of sixteen different nationalities including Russian, Serbian, Hungarian, Belgian, Austrian and even a few Latin Americans had passed through by the end of the war. The Governor in his Annual Report to the Commissioners for the year, 1917, comments that his charges came not only from a variety of races but from all strata of society – from ex-officers to ex-convicts. Friction was inevitable and the staff were continually obliged to exercise the greatest of tact and diplomacy to avoid trouble between factions.

The internees were not obliged to work although many were quite thankful for the opportunity to do so in order to pass the time. The variety of employment was not great, mailbag sewing being the usual task. A number of men were also employed as cleaners, gardeners and in the laundry. Those whose performance was satisfactory could earn as much as 14s. per week, a sum far in excess of the pay of the soldier in the front line. The earnings could be saved, spent in the canteen or used for the purchase of unrationed foodstuffs and the like which could be ordered from local shops.

Having regard to the shortage of food which was experienced by the civilian population from 1916, the scale of diet for the internees was generous and varied. Breakfast comprised a pint of porridge with bread and margarine and the choice of tea or coffee. A typical week's dinner menu:

Monday	Soup (with 3 oz. clods), vegetables, potatoes
Tuesday	Fish, 12 oz., rice, potatoes, pudding
Wednesday	Salt pork, 1½ oz., beans, potatoes, fruit
Thursday	Beef, 6 oz., potatoes
Friday	Vegetable soup, 1 pt, peas, potatoes
Saturday	Fish, 12 oz., potatoes, tapioca, 3 oz., jam, 2 oz.

For supper the internee would be served bread and margarine, potatoes and cheese together with a pint of tea or coffee.

The comparative peace of the establishment was rudely shattered in July 1916, by the arrival of a group of 37 Sinn Fein supporters the bulk of whom had been taken into custody following the Easter insurrection in Dublin. It would seem that the authorities were uncertain as to whether these men were to be treated as criminals or as political prisoners but as so often is the case a compromise was found. It was accordingly ordered that whilst these men were to be treated as inmates of a local prison they were to be allowed certain extra privileges. Like the internees, the Irish, who were housed in E Wing, the former women's prison, were to be allowed unlimited association between the hours of 7 a.m. and 8 p.m., they were permitted to smoke and could arrange for unrationed foodstuffs and goods to be purchased on their behalf. Their diet, too, was similar to that allowed the internees. They were, on the other hand, allowed neither to receive nor to send letters. Visits likewise were forbidden. With the exception of a handful of men who were transferred elsewhere within a week or two of their arrival in Reading, this group were repatriated on Christmas Eve 1916.

It is not known how the Irish spent their Christmas but for the aliens their Christmas menu was:

Bread	Hot mutton
Potatoes	Peas or beans

Pudding.

For those who were prepared to meet the cost from their own pocket there was roast pork and stuffing. A little wine was served with the meal and beer could be purchased.

A further group of Irish prisoners arrived during the spring and summer of 1918. Militants to a man, many of them had been involved in a mutiny at Lewes Prison. By this time the shortage of prison staff was acute and the Governor was to experience grave anxiety. Could any disturbance or mutiny be contained? There being rumours of a work and hunger strike it was arranged for Special Constables to augment the staff for patrol duties during the evenings.

Numbered among the Irish detainees was William Cosgrave who, having survived a death sentence imposed for his part in the Easter rising, went on to become Chairman of the Provisional Government of 1922 and subsequently President of the Executive Council of the Free State. Following the 1932 election he gave way to Eamonn de Valera and served as Leader of the Opposition until his retirement in 1944.

An internee who had already made his name in Irish politics and who came to Reading with the second group was Laurence Ginnell, Member of Parliament for Westmeath. Fiery and argumentative, one could be sure that if there was trouble, Larry Ginnell had a hand in it. He knew the law and exercised his rights to the full. In a report to the Prison Commissioners, the Governor, Captain Morgan says of him:

The man who is most offensive is L. Ginnell but his reputation is doubtless known to the Commissioners without any comment of mine. He must either be taken seriously or ignored – I prefer the latter and act on it but I am not at all sure that the Visiting Committee will stand his remarks when they visit him. He has called a few men round him much like himself. I refer the Commissioners to the fact that the men sent to Reading had mutinied elsewhere and that they anticipate trouble from them in this prison.

There was in fact no mutiny. The Irish remaining within the law were provocative in the extreme and one person who witnessed their departure with relief was the Steward (the member of staff responsible for the day-to-day administration of the prison and who is today known as the Administration Officer) who, temporarily quartered in the Chaplain's residence, complained that any noise from within E Wing could be plainly heard. In his own words: 'The Irish prisoners give us little peace between 7 a.m. and 10 p.m. There is shouting and cheering, drilling, chorus singing, violin and flute playing with much walking up and down stairs.'

As the war dragged on life for both internees and staff became far from easy. Fears for the safety of relatives and friends at the battle front or for families far away on the ravaged Continent brought tempers all too often near to boiling point. A Warder who had lost a son in France could not find it easy to be civil to the Germans in his charge. The food shortage with which the civilian population had to contend was felt in the prison also. The shortage of potatoes following the bad harvest of 1916 brought about a reduction in the quantity of food served whilst the bread, its flour diluted with barley or oatmeal in order to conserve wheat, was coarse, dark and dry.

September 1917 brought heavy air raids upon London and as a safety measure the windows in the domed ceiling above the central hall were blacked out with a mixture of oil and lamp-black. These skylight panes being an important source of illumination, the wings must have been gloomy indeed. The remaining windows were obscured with curtains improvised from blankets.

The insatiable demands of the armed forces for manpower reduced the strength of the Prison Service to a point at which it was almost impossible to staff the prisons. Hours were long and pay was quite inadequate to meet the rising prices without hardship. Those Warders who were obliged to work away from home were poorly compensated. A letter dated 11 September 1918 from Warder W. J. Maddock, an officer who was transferred from his home in Liverpool to Portland and later to Reading illustrates the situation with great clarity:

To the Governor,

Sir,

I humbly appeal whilst I am on special duty at the above address that I may be allowed to receive 3s. per day from minimum Separation Allowance, the same as granted me by the Prison Commissioners at Portland Prison when lodging in that prison. Owing to the excess increase in cost of living it is impossible to get proper sustenance at 2s. per day.

I am, Sir, your obedient servant,

W. J. MADDOCK

Hostilities ceased on 11 November 1918. Within His Majesty's Place of Internment there was thanksgiving but little rejoicing. For many of the internees the future seemed to have little to offer. For internees and staff alike there were the same scarcity of food and shortage of necessaries to be endured whilst prices remained unbelievably high. There was little warmth and light to be enjoyed that winter.

With the New Year, authorization for the release of wartime detainees began to arrive. For those who wished to leave England, arrangements were made for repatriation. A few were to remain in England, their personal particulars recorded as required by the Aliens Act, but otherwise unmolested. By the end of 1919 they had gone their separate ways leaving behind no trace of four years' cosmopolitan occupation.

11 THE MODERN PRISON

The last of the Irish detainees returned to their homeland in March 1919, and by the end of the year those aliens who had not been repatriated were released to settle in the United Kingdom. When the Visiting Committee met on 24 January 1920, there were no prisoners in custody and no indication had been given by the Commissioners as to when the services of the establishment would again be required. The meeting was accordingly adjourned *sine die*. By June, the Governor, Capt. Morgan, assisted by a skeleton staff, had wound up the affairs of H.M. Place of Internment and had departed.

Between the wars the body of the prison stood empty while grass and weeds flourished in the yards and gardens. The building was not however derelict, a caretaker calling from time to time to ensure that all was well. That the gaol was not serving its accustomed function did not escape the notice of the citizens of the town and from time to time letters appeared in the local Press suggesting that the site be put to more profitable use. Why not convert this pseudo-baronial hall into blocks of flats, they asked? Why not rebuild it as an hotel? The corporation, too, coveted the site. So conveniently placed near the centre of the town, here was the ideal location for a new civic centre. But the Prison Commissioners were adamant in their refusal to consider any such suggestion.

By 1935, the Governor's residence had been let to the War Department for use as an Army Recruiting Office whilst the Insurance Department of the Ministry of Health and the local office of the Ministry of Pensions were established in the Chaplain's house. Kelly's Directory of Reading for that year shows the three corner turrets in private occupation. The Governor's house was subsequently fitted up as the Regional A.R.P. Commission Headquarters. This was to have been the Control Centre but about the time of the Munich Crisis this plan was deemed impracticable. Following the outbreak of war in 1939, the Deputy Governor of Feltham Borstal came with a working party to clean the premises and to prepare them for wartime use. It is believed that it was the intention of the Government to use the prison for the custody of enemy aliens and Fifth Columnists and a former Governor tells that a portable gallows was erected in the yard. One is however inclined to doubt this statement as in D Wing there was a suite of two condemned cells together with a perfectly serviceable execution shed complete with drop apparatus. The *Reading Chronicle* of 12 July 1946, records that early in the war a minor mystery was created by the arrival at the prison shortly before dusk every evening of a party of men. It was later revealed that the men were in fact prisoners from Wormwood Scrubs drafted in for fire-watching duty.

In August 1940, a party of lads who had survived the bombing of Portland Borstal were transferred to Reading under the Governorship of Sir Almeric Rich. They remained in occupation until 19 October when 29 of them were transferred in two buses to Sherwood. Six lads who were due to be discharged within the next couple of weeks were left behind to clear up.

Hardly had the Borstal lads departed when the prison was commandeered by the military authorities and handed over to the Canadian Army for use as a military detention prison. Little is known of the number of soldiers detained or of the regime at that time but one of the few local persons able to gain admittance recalls the strange and disturbing sight of guards armed with sub-machine guns patrolling the landings of an English prison.

The crime wave of the early post-war years with the resultant demand for prison accommodation caused the Prison Commissioners to reopen Reading prison which had been vacated by the Army in 1945. On 19 August 1946, Mr W. P. Harding arrived to take up the post of Governor of what was to be an 'overflow' prison for men sentenced to short terms of imprisonment. The building having been made ready and the necessary staff drafted in, the first batch of 24 prisoners was received from Winson Green on 24 September.

Among the reforms introduced by the Criminal Justice Act of 1948 was the sentence of Corrective Training. It was at last recognized that there was little profit to be gained by merely removing the young recidivist from society and the new legislation offered remedial training over a period of from 2 – 4 years for certain offenders aged from 21 to 30 years. In order that the system should not become clogged with persons unfitted for such training it was decided to set up an assessment centre at which men sent for Corrective Training could be sent for observation, interview and aptitude testing. Reading Prison was selected for this important role and the first Corrective Trainees were received on 15 December 1949. The wisdom of the prison authorities in setting up the allocation machinery is witnessed in the Governor's first annual report on the working of the Centre; 'a not inconsiderable number (of trainees) would have been reported unsuitable if the evidence subsequently obtained at Reading had been available at the time of the trial'. In the Prison Commissioners' Report for 1951 it is revealed that of the men who had passed through the Centre up to the end of that year, some 16 per cent had either been previously certified as insane or had received treatment at some time in mental hospitals. The conjoint weaknesses of the lack of a reliable assessment prior to sentence as to trainability and the tendency of some Courts to use Corrective Training as a means of imposing a longer sentence than would otherwise have been legal, stood revealed.

The function of the establishment again changed in 1951. Early in December of that year the last of the Corrective Trainees moved on and a few days later the prison was designated a Borstal Institution. The Borstal system provides an alternative to imprisonment for offenders aged from 16 to 21 years; the course of training is geared to prepare the Trainee for a full and useful life in the community. The period of training is indeterminate within the limitations of a minimum term of 6 months and a maximum of 2 years and the length of time served in custody is determined by the progress of the individual. Within the system the various institutions have their special role – some are closed and cater for the more disturbed and unruly element who require fairly secure conditions, while others are open and afford the minimum of restraint. Some institutions offer courses of training in technical and craft subjects while others are concerned with agriculture. Certain specialist Borstal Institutions provide remedial education or medical and psychiatric care. The role of Reading within the scheme was that of Correctional and Recall Centre. Boys who at Training Borstals offended against discipline and good order or who absconded were sent to Reading to experience a period of 'correction' before being sent on to another establishment. To Reading also came young men who, having been released subject to a period of compulsory supervision, had committed further offences and were ordered by the Court to be returned for additional training. It was required that the regime should embody firmness and deterrence but yet should be positive in content. Privileges were reduced to a minimum, the work was hard and high standards of discipline and cleanliness were demanded at all times. Among Borstal trainees, Reading had a reputation to be feared.

On Sunday 17 September 1967, the *People* newspaper carried a lurid front page article entitled 'Brutality at a Borstal' alleging inhumane treatment of the boys at Reading Borstal by members of the staff. Among the many complaints were allegations that members of the staff had slapped and even beaten recalcitrant trainees and that others had been forced into baths of near scalding water. The Prison Department which since Du Cane's day has been notoriously sensitive to even the slightest hint of criticism by the Press or in Parliament, acted quickly and within a week a five man Board of Enquiry was set up to look into the matter. The Board held its initial meeting on 25 September and on 10 October began its investigations in earnest. The enquiry was full and searching with both Officers and boys being called upon to give evidence. The Board sat regularly until 28 December when its findings were submitted to the Home Office.

On 6 March 1968, the Home Secretary, Mr Callaghan, in a written reply to a Parliamentary question stated that the Board of Enquiry had unanimously concluded that there was substance in the allegations of irregular behaviour by certain Officers. He went on to say that the Board had found difficulty in establishing the truth of the matter because of the unreliability of some of the witnesses but it was clear that a certain pattern of behaviour had grown up over several years among some of the Officers who believed that discipline should be imposed by force rather than by personality and example. These malpractices, said Mr Callaghan, had now stopped. He concluded by saying that the Borstal would close and that the establishment would revert to a prison role.

No further trainees were received into the Correctional Centre and by early May the last of the lads who had been transferred in on that basis had been moved elsewhere. During the remainder of the year the establishment functioned as a Recall Centre and accepted only lads who had failed following release on Licence and who had been returned for further training. In order to demonstrate that whatever had happened before all was now well, an Open Day was held in October 1968, the guest of honour being the Mayor of Reading. The Directors of the Prison Service and of the Borstal Administration and no fewer than 178 guests attended to view the premises, to witness a demonstration of gymnastics by the boys and to see them beat the staff at volleyball. Morale was again high.

The Borstal finally closed on 14 January 1969, the last of the boys being released on that date. The following day the establishment was reclassified as a prison. Plans had by this time been drawn up for a complete modernization of the premises. Utilizing prison labour so far as was practicable it was proposed to refurbish the interior of the building. New work was to include a complex comprising workshops, kitchen and dining hall. A new office block to house the administrative staff and to provide facilities for visiting was also proposed. The boundary wall was to be renewed, the existing Gate Lodge being replaced by a structure of modern design. The planning authorities demanded that the external appearance of the building should remain unchanged so far as was possible although it was accepted that the cell windows must of necessity be replaced and frames of a pattern designed to pass the maximum of light and fresh air consistent with security fitted.

In early February, the first group of adult prisoners arrived to assist with the preliminaries to rebuilding.

Within the building the first major operation was the removal of Haden's boilers (which had operated very efficiently for over a century) and the construction of a modern oil-fired boiler installation in the area beneath the Central Hall. The boiler house having been completed there arose the problem of taking five separate flues through the interior of the building to the central turret. Due to the solidity of the original fabric and to the confined spaces in which the builders had to operate, there were many problems to be overcome. The task was accomplished by use of preformed concrete units encased in brickwork to roof level and from there upwards in steel.

The red and black tiled floors in the wings and cells were taken up and replaced with concrete. The doors and windows of each cell were replaced creating an effect of spaciousness without any alteration to the dimensions. The electrical system was renewed in its entirety and each cell provided with a fluorescent striplight which the prisoner could himself operate. From the point of view of comfort and health one of the more important modifications was the installation of efficient and hygienic toilet and bathing facilities.

At the same time as the modernization of the main building was progressing, demolition work was going on outside. With the exception of one workshop, all the outbuildings were swept away to make room for a spacious two-storey building extending from the angle between A and B Wings to the southern boundary wall. When complete there will be ample workshop space for two or more industries. On the upper floor will be a modern kitchen and dining-room. Access to this complex from the main building will be by way of a bridge from the southern extremity of B Wing.

It was intended that major constructional work should be undertaken by a civilian contractor and tenders for the workshop building and new gate lodge were sought in the normal way. The contract was awarded to Messrs Emery of High Wycombe, a small firm of building contractors. Whilst the standard of workmanship appears to have been very satisfactory the scale of the project proved too demanding for the financial resources available and on 29 September 1972, operations ceased. Following a lengthy delay whilst the completed work was measured and a settlement negotiated, it was decided that the Works Department of the Prison Department should be nominated main contractor and the remainder of the work carried out so far as was possible by inmate labour. Although progress since this time has been less rapid than would have been the case had another firm of building contractors been engaged, the results appear equally satisfactory and the opportunity for prisoners to learn the skills necessary for future employment in the building trade or for those already trained to keep in practice has proved beneficial to a considerable number of men.

In October 1971, the former female wing became redundant, its occupants having moved into A Wing to occupy cells which they had themselves renovated and redecorated. Once again the demolition team was brought into action and for a few days the interior of the building was exposed to persons passing along Forbury Road affording many of them their first and only sight of the interior of a prison. At the same time the former Governor's and Chaplain's residences flanking the main gate were pulled down. At the time of writing (November 1973) the miniature barbican still stands but will shortly give way to the new gate lodge with its electrically operated sliding gate which looks for all the world like a blockhouse from Hitler's Atlantic Wall. In its place will stand an office block to house the not inconsiderable staff of clerks and typists without whom no Government establishment can function.

Whilst the site for the new gate lodge was being cleared, Mr T. Gwatkin, the Director of the Borough Museum and Art Gallery, seized the opportunity to carry out an archaeological investigation of the site. It was known that the prison sits over the east end of the Abbey Church of which fragments survive. The last opportunity for excavation came to an end in 1843 when the boundary wall was erected. It was hoped that the foundations of the east end of the Abbey Church, the site of the High Altar and of the Lady Chapel, might be exposed. In the event, the excavation unearthed neither of these but brought to light for the first time one and a part of another of what is believed to be a set of three chapels. The chapel which was discovered was about 12 ft in width with a semi-circular apse. As only foundations remained there were few finds of pottery or other artifacts. An area of decorated floor tiles was however uncovered and lifted for preservation by members of the Museum staff.

Although the legend has long been discounted, one suspects that the archaeologists engaged on the site cherished secret hopes that they might discover the silver coffin in which the remains of Henry II are said to have been laid to rest. Unfortunately, no trace was found of the High Altar beneath which the tomb was believed to lie, nor was there any indication of the site of the Lady Chapel.

A contributor to the *Gentlemen's Magazine* of January 1786, writing under the pseudonym 'Juvenis' relates how in the previous year workmen digging the foundation trenches of the House of Correction discovered, on the spot where the old abbey stood, a vault of curious workmanship containing a leaden coffin almost devoured by time in which was enclosed a perfect skeleton. From the distinguished appearance of the vault, of the coffin and more particularly from fragments of rotten leather found with the remains, it was thought that the royal burial place had been discovered. It having been said that the body of the king was wrapped in oxhides prior to burial, the presence of leather in the coffin was deemed conclusive evidence until a more thorough examination revealed that the supposed oxhide was in reality nothing more than fragments of a decayed slipper.

The remains of the buildings connected with the abbey having been largely swept away during the rebuilding operations of 1791 and 1842, little of value was discovered when the site was recently laid bare in readiness for the erection of the workshop buildings. Portions of the flint foundations of the abbey which had lain hitherto undisturbed were from time to time encountered during the course of piling work and the capabilities of modern drilling equipment were severely tested.

The prison site encroaches upon the cemetery of the Hospitium of the abbey. The greater part of the remains there interred were removed in 1791 but a number of human skeletons were discovered. Also unearthed was a pit containing a jumble of bones. This was thought at first to be a plague pit but reference to early records has disclosed that the builders of the old gaol disposed in this way of the bones which they had uncovered.

The present role of the prison is to cater for the type of prisoner who may best be described as socially inadequate – the man in the larger prison who, either by the nature of his offence or by his conduct whilst in custody, has found himself rejected and ostracized by his fellows. At the present time there are some 70 inmates of this category in residence but the number will rise to nearly 200 when the rebuilding project is complete. This special category of prisoner has little contact with those brought in to work as building tradesmen. There is, however, little friction, if any, between the two classes.

The process to which the inmate is subjected today is one of re-education, the aim of which is to change his outlook and behaviour by example, persuasion and by the inculcation of a degree of self-awareness. It has brought into the prison a variety of new officers: psychologists, psychiatrists, education officers, teachers and welfare officers, most of whom are still regarded rather warily by those well-established, older members of the Prison Service who are more accustomed to traditional methods and are uncertain of the value of specialized techniques. The value of the members of the uniformed staff who, one must not forget, see a great deal more of the prisoners and come to know them better in all their moods, than any of the specialists, is not overlooked. Not only are the Officers encouraged to take an interest in the personalities and problems of the prisoners in their charge, they are required also to take an active part in case discussion and decision-making.

Whilst it cannot be claimed that the system at present in operation even approaches perfection, the pursuit of the spirit of Rule 1 of The Prison Rules, namely: 'The purpose of the training and treatment of convicted prisoners shall be to encourage and assist them to lead a good and useful life' is being undertaken more wholeheartedly and enthusiastically than at any time in the past.

APPENDIX I
Governors of Reading Gaol

1792 – 1815	Mr G. Knight
1815 – 1826	Mr George Eastaff
1826 – 1834	Mr Thomas Eastaff
1835 – 1853	Lieut E. Hackett, RN
1854 – 1876	Mr S. Ferry
1877 – 1878	Col W. L. Randall
1882 – 1887	Capt. C. A. Blythe
1890 – 1896	Lieut-Col H. B. Isaacson
1896 – 1899	Maj. J. B. Nelson
1899 – 1902	Capt. C. W. B. Farrant
1903 – 1905	Capt. R. H. D'aeth
1905 – 1906	Capt. S. F. Judge, DSO
1908 – 1913	Capt. T. F. M. Wisden
1913 – 1920	Capt. C. M. Morgan

The prison stood empty between the years 1920 – 1939

1939	Mr T. W. Hayes
1940	Sir Almeric Rich

Between the latter months of 1940 and 1945 the prison was subject to Canadian military control

1946 – 1949	Mr W. P. Harding
1949 – 1950	Mr D. W. G. Malone
1950 – 1954	Mr G. B. Smith
1954 – 1958	Mr E. E. Gregory
1958 – 1962	Mr F. V. Elvey
1962 – 1966	Mr N. C. Honey
1966 – 1971	Mr L. A. Portch
1972 –	Mr A. R. Richards

APPENDIX II
Executions at the County Gaol since 1800

6 March 1800	John Hutt	Murder of Ann Pearman
16 July 1801	James Dormer	Murder of Mr Robinson
29 March 1802	John Ryan	Murder of Henry Frewin at Birchett's Green
29 March 1802	Edward Painter	Theft of two heifers from Mortimer Fair
19 March 1803	Dennis Daly	Forging cheque for £10
23 March 1811	Thomas Cox (20)	Bestiality
26 March 1814	Charles White	Horse stealing
25 March 1815	John Newbank (or Newcombe)	Uttering forged notes
2 August 1817	James Castle	Sheep stealing at Abingdon
15 July 1817	Thomas Ayres	Housebreaking with violence, Sulhampstead Abbotts
7 August 1819	Edward Tooley ⎫ David Patience ⎬	Housebreaking at Langford
18 March 1820	George Wiggins	Robbery at Thatcham
4 March 1824	Daniel Grimshire	Murder of his infant son
28 May 1824	William Giles	Uttering forged £5 note

22 March 1828	Henry Burnett Thomas Field Samuel White	Shooting a keeper whilst poaching
11 January 1831	William Winterbourne	Robbery; complicity in agricultural riots
25 February 1833	John Carter	Arson at Lambourne
4 August 1833	Edward Green Thomas Lincoln James Morris	Burglary
3 March 1834	George King (19)	Murder of Mrs Ann Pullin, landlady of 'The White Hart', Wantage
20 March 1835	William Spicer	Basket maker of Howard Street, Reading, convicted of the murder of his wife by beating her about the head with a poker
22 March 1844	Thomas Jennings	Murder by poison of his son aged 4 years
14 March 1862	John Gould	Murder of his daughter aged 7 years by cut- ting her throat with a razor. Reading's last public execution

12 March 1877	Henry Tidbury Francis Tidbury }	Murder of P.C. Drewitt and Insp. Shorter at Hungerford
5 December 1893	John Carter	Murder of his third wife at Watchfield. Also believed to have murdered his second wife
7 July 1896	Charles Thomas Wooldridge	Murder of his wife at Clewer. The subject of Oscar Wilde's 'The Ballad of Reading Gaol'
28 November 1899	Charles Scott	Murder of Eliza O'Shea at Windsor
5 November 1907	William George Austin	Murder of Unity Alice Butler at Clewer
24 November 1910	William Broome	Murder of elderly woman shopkeeper at Slough
4 February 1913	Eric James Sedgwick	Murder of young woman at Eton College

BIBLIOGRAPHY

ANON.,   *The life of Charles White, 1814.*

ANON.,   *Reading seventy years ago; a record of events from 1813–1819, 1887.*

BRESSLER, F.,   *Reprieve,* Harrap, 1965.

CROSS, RUPERT,   *Punishment, prison and the public,* Stevens, 1971.

ELKIN, W. A.,   *The English penal system,* Penguin, 1957.

FIELD, THE REV. J., *The life of John Howard,* Longman, Brown & Co., 1850.

——   *Prison discipline, 1846.*

FLETCHER, WILLIAM, *Reading past and present, 1838.*

FOX, SIR LIONEL,   *The modern English prison,* Routledge, 1934.

HALDAR, RAKHAL DAS, *The English diary of an Indian student,* Dacca, Asutosh Library, 1903.

HOME OFFICE,   *People in prison,* H.M.S.O., 1969.

HOWARD, JOHN,   *The state of the prisons in England and Wales, 1778.*

HURRY, J. B.,   *Reading Abbey, 1901.*

HYDE, H. MONTGOMERY, *Oscar Wilde : the aftermath,* Methuen, 1963.

——   *The trials of Oscar Wilde* (Notable British Trials Series), Hodge, 1948.

JONES, JOHN B.,   *Sketches of Reading – 1870, 1870.*

JULLIAN, P.,   *Oscar Wilde,* Constable, 1969.

KERRY, THE REV. C., *A history of the municipal church of St Lawrence, Reading, 1883.*

KLARE, HUGH,   *People in prison,* Pitman, 1973.

MAN, JOHN,   *The history and antiquities of the borough of Reading, 1816.*

——   *The stranger in Reading, 1810.*

MILTON, F.,   *The English magistracy,* Oxford University Press, 1967.

'OCTOGENARIAN',   *Reminiscences of Reading,* 1888.

PLAYFAIR, GILES,   *The punitive obsession,* Gollancz, 1971.

SPRIGGS, F. G.,   *History of the church of Greyfriars, Reading,* 1963.

THOMAS, J. E.,   *The English prison officer since 1850,* Routledge and Kegan Paul, 1972.

WEBB, BEATRICE and SIDNEY,   *English prisons under local government,* Longman, 1922.

WILDE, OSCAR,   *De Profundis,* posthumous publication with preface by Robert Ross, 1905.

——   *The Ballad of Reading Gaol,* Leonard Smithers, 1898.

WYKES, ALAN,   *Reading,* Macmillan, 1970.

INDEX